The
Environment
Equation

D1005045

First published in North America by Adams Media, an F+W Publications Company
57 Littlefield Street
Avon, MA 02322
www.adamsmedia.com

Conceived and produced by
Elwin Street Productions
144 Liverpool Road
London N1 1LA
www.elwinstreet.com

ISBN 10: 1-59869-814-1
ISBN 13: 978-1-59869-814-5

Layouts designed by Louise Leffler

Picture credits: Corbis: 28, 70, 78, 88, 104; Dreamstime: 43, 45, 63, 87, 74, 76, 83, 96, 101, 103, 106; iStock photos: 12, 33, 46, 48, 52, 55, 57, 59, 67, 69, 72, 86, 91, 94, 98, 102, 108, 110, 112, 113, 115, 117, 119, 120, 123, 125, 126, 129, 134, 137; Photolibrary: 50; Shutterstock: 11, 14, 19, 22, 24, 34, 36.

Printed in Singapore
J I H G F E D C B A

This publication is designed to provide accurate and authoritative information with regard to the subject matter covered. It is sold with the understanding that the publisher is not engaged in rendering legal, accounting, or other professional advice. If legal advice or other expert assistance is required, the services of a competent professional person should be sought.
—From a Declaration of Principles jointly adopted by a Committee of the American Bar Association and a Committee of Publishers and Associations

Many of the designations used by manufacturers and sellers to distinguish their product are claimed as trademarks. Where those designations appear in the book and Adams Media was aware of a trademark claim, the designations have been printed with initial capital letters.

This book is available at quantity discounts for bulk purchases.
For information, please call 1-800-289-0963.

The
Environment
Equation

Alex Shimo-Barry
with Christopher J. Maron

Aadamsmedia

Contents

Introduction

"In the future, everybody will want to do the right thing!" is what a Nature Conservancy colleague exclaimed at a meeting in 1991 to discuss involving the public more in efforts to save nature and preserve life. When I walked through a local bookstore last week, it hit me that the future is now! Arrayed on tables was a large assortment of books catering to people's desire to do the "environmental" right thing.

My first thought when I saw these books was to question the need for books to tell people how to live simpler, more environmentally-friendly lives. Much of that information is obvious—consume less, eat local food, recycle, get fuel-efficient cars, turn off lights, insulate, and wear sweaters in winter. Yet, even after doing these simple things, people may wonder how much of an effect it really has in the bigger picture.

Now, with *The Environment Equation* you can get mathematical values for reducing your carbon footprint and being a good environmental citizen. You could start with figuring the savings of turning off lights when you are not home. See how much that is for a year and then consider the total when a million people do that. Then do it-that simple act makes you part of a global solution because your actions mean something.

You will see benefits from other actions; like the 4,400 fewer pounds of carbon dioxide released per year when you dump the SUV for a smaller car. Buying local food does you even better because you will save 5,000 pounds of carbon dioxide from being emitted. By reading this book, you can reduce your carbon footprint, estimate what effect your actions will have, and then chart your participation in saving our world.

The book may inspire you to discover other ways to reduce carbon use. For example, as I read the chapter about "Greener Consumption," I thought of how parents can feed their children in a more sustainable way; breast-feeding reduces the need to produce, package, transport, and heat up formula. Or, instead of buying jars of baby food, get a food grinder designed to convert adult food to a mush for little mouths.

I recently read a newspaper article about students demanding more action to reduce carbon use in their schools and outside, where parents sit in idling cars that spew out CO_2 and pollutants. Because children are the future, it is important to provide them with ideas and convincing information to encourage changes that will sustain our planet.

Back in 1991, when we heard the exclamation about people in the future wanting to do the right thing, we realized that we were struggling then to have people embrace land conservation; yet over time, people would naturally become more aware of our planet's plight, realize that individual actions are effective, find ways to measure their efforts, and do the right thing. That has happened and now, with *The Environment Equation*, they can act, calculate their progress in living green, and play a role in saving our world.

Christopher J. Maron, Champlain Valley Program Director
for The Nature Conservancy, Adirondack (NY) chapter

How to use this book

The consequences of climate change are expected to fundamentally alter the health and diversity of life around the world. The choices and actions we take today will help shape what type of future we give the next generation. Each of us can work towards a solution by reducing the size of our carbon footprint. This book gives you a step-by-step guide on how to do this, and what the effect of your actions will be.

On the next page you'll find a carbon calculator so that you can figure out the size of your carbon footprint. The following pages identify easy steps you can take to reduce this figure. All the suggested ideas have been carefully evaluated in terms of practicality and cost. The impact of each action has also been calculated, measured in pounds of carbon dioxide per year. Add or subtract the amount of carbon dioxide for each entry as they apply to your lifestyle, and you'll get an idea of just how much carbon you could save.

These calculations are based on the latest studies in this area. Because we all do things in different ways, carbon emissions vary according to the person, where they live, how they live, and many other factors. The numbers in this book are

meant as a guide for action, rather than exact calculations. Nevertheless, we hope these figures will raise awareness about how simple changes can play an important role shaping the future of our planet.

Carbon calculator

On average, Americans release 20 tons of CO_2 per year, and Europeans 12 tons. Calculate your current yearly carbon footprint with the information below:

A) Electricity at home: Multiply your monthly electricity bill by 105

B) Heating at home: Multiply your monthly gas bill by 105

C) Fuel oil at home: Multiply your monthly fuel oil bill by 113

D) Your car's mileage: Multiply total yearly mileage by 7.9

E) Flights (Short–medium haul—less than 4 hours): Multiply the number of flights by 1,100 lbs

F) Flights (Long haul—more than 4 hours): Multiply the number of flights by 4,400 lbs

G) Recycling: Do you recycle newspaper? If no, add 184 lbs. If yes, add 0

H) Recycling: Do you recycle aluminum and tin cans? If no, add 166 lbs. If yes, add 0

How do you measure up

Total: A + B + C + D + E + F + G + H

Below 6000 lbs/yr	Excellent	(Note: This calculation presumes a one-
6000–15,999 lbs/yr	Good	person household—if there is more than
16,000–22,000 lbs/yr	Average	one person, then divide A, B and C by the
Over 22,000 lbs/yr	Poor	number of adults in the household.)

Interested in preventing this planet's meltdown? Your home is the best place to start. Our houses are responsible for about 20 percent of the carbon emissions released each year. Not only that, but carbon emissions from buildings and the construction industry are predicted to grow faster than from any other sector of the economy, including heavy industry and automobiles.

The good news is that many of the changes described in the following pages will save you money in the long run. The best way to emit less carbon is to save energy, and less energy means less money spent on your utility bills. You may want to take action but don't necessarily have money to burn on expensive environmental investments (although if you do, even better). So each of the following ideas have been evaluated in terms of cost, convenience, and the impact they will make on your individual carbon emissions.

Should you decide to make changes to your home, many governments now provide incentives to encourage people to reduce their energy consumption as part of their climate change program. In the United States, investment incentives are usually in the form of tax credits and grants. The Database of State Incentives for Renewables & Efficiency is a comprehensive source on state, local, and federal initiatives that promote renewable energy and energy efficiency.

PART ONE

Dream Home

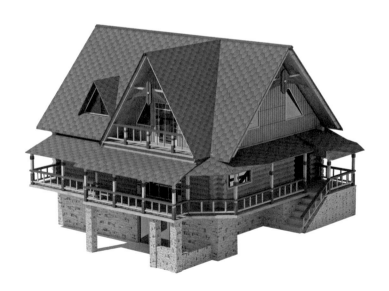

New carpets

15 lbs

CO_2 per square yard

If all men are created equal, all carpets certainly are not. You can now buy carpets that are environmentally friendly, where the company has used recycled materials or made a commitment to reducing its carbon emissions. Most of the carbon emissions from the lifecycle of a carpet for example are released during the course of extraction and processing of the raw materials.

Environmental accreditation (having the products labelled as eco-friendly), is making progress in the commercial sector, but the residential sector has not kept up. Residential carpets often don't have any independent green standards to identify them as environmentally friendly, although that doesn't necessarily mean that they are not. You may have to do your own sleuthing when shopping for a floor covering that doesn't harm the environment. Look for carpets that are made to last a long time and are made from recycled materials. The polyester yarn PET, for example, is made from plastic soda bottles and has a higher percentage of recycled fiber than any other fabric. Since it is naturally stain resistant, it does not require heavy chemical treatments. Carpets made from nylon—either nylon 6 or nylon 6.6—can also be recycled.

Keep in mind that the amount of recycled material does not necessarily indicate how environmentally friendly the company. As the carpet company gets more efficient at working with used materials, the amount of recycled fabric needed will drop. It's also worth choosing companies that collect old carpets once they are worn out. They will not only recycle the fabrics, they'll also save space in the garbage dump.

If you decide on a natural material, such as grasses, cotton, or wool, they won't be recycled, since they biodegrade as they wear. However, natural fabrics that haven't received much chemical treatment are quite often just as environmentally friendly. For example, wool carpets are naturally flame resistant and durable, and they provide excellent indoor environmental quality, albeit at a higher price. PLA, a corn-based carpet, does not release many greenhouse gases in its production, says Firth, although it does not last as long as wool. Hemp carpets are strong, durable, and they make great compost once you throw them out.

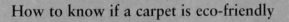

How to know if a carpet is eco-friendly

• Carpets that are environmentally friendly may be certified by an independent environmental organization, such as Smart Certified. This measures a product's carbon footprint and impact on the environment. Products are awarded silver, gold and platinum accreditation.

• A commercial carpet that's doesn't reach these standards will release about 34 lbs of CO_2 per square yard. A really green carpet will release up to 40 percent less global warming gases. This is because the company has committed to using recycled content and renewable power supplies, and investing in more efficient technologies.

Microwave

55 lbs

CO$_2$ per year

A microwave can be a very convenient tool in the kitchen, and while not suitable for all types of cooking, microwaves are extremely efficient, saving time as well as energy and carbon emissions. Since they really only warm the food instead of the whole oven, a study done by the American Council for an Energy Efficient Economy estimates that they use two-thirds less energy than cooking in a conventional oven, so if you are able to do a quarter of your cooking in the microwave you could save 55 lbs a year.

Although there are many dishes that can't be prepared in a microwave, some foods are particularly well-suited for the appliance. You could use it to steam vegetables, cook potatoes in about five minutes (just 60 seconds per potato), and boil water with a quick zap if you are in a hurry. Although there have been some concerns about whether microwaves might cause cancer, decades of research

have not produced a definitive link, and the American Cancer Society and Cancer Research UK both agree that there is no need to worry. In the summer months, cooking with smaller appliances such as microwaves and toaster ovens can help keep cooling and air conditioning costs down, since ovens tend to heat the whole kitchen and adjacent rooms. And if you clean your microwave regularly and don't allow the splatter stains to build up, it will cook more efficiently too.

Energy audit

1,000 lbs ▬

CO_2 per year

Are you wasting energy? The average American releases about 20 metric tons of carbon dioxide into the atmosphere each year. China currently releases 3.84 metric per person, although with a billion people its total emissions are the largest in the world. Europeans do a little better at 12 metric tons per individual.

Wherever you live, one of the biggest sources of these carbon emissions is your home. Residential buildings account for about one fifth of our total carbon emissions. This sector is growing, largely because power usage is strongly linked to the weather. With higher summer temperatures, air conditioning use rises, causing electricity use to surge.

One of the best ways to find out how to shrink your carbon footprint is an energy audit. You can either do this yourself, by looking for air leaks (see entry 4) or checking whether you are spending more on your utility bills than you should (there's lots of information on the web about how to make these household comparisons). Or, you could have an audit done by the experts. This usually makes good business sense as most utility providers will do it free of charge. Professional auditors will find those hard-to-detect energy losses by using a variety of specialist equipment, such as blower doors and infrared cameras, which can pinpoint exactly how your house is losing heat.

Of course, once you've had an audit, you still need to implement their suggestions before you start making energy savings. But at least you'll know where you can make a difference.

Air leaks

800 lbs

CO_2 per year

On average, you can cut your heating bill by almost a third by weatherizing your home. Hidden air leaks cause some of the largest heat losses, especially in older homes. You can hire an energy auditor to help you find these gaps, or you can find them yourself using just a stick of incense.

Hold the lit stick next to windows, doors, electrical boxes, plumbing fixtures, electrical outlets, ceiling fixtures, attic hatches, and other locations where there is a possible air path to the outside. When the smoke stream travels horizontally, there is an air leak that needs to be caulked.

The best material for sealing these hidden air leaks depends on the size of the gaps and where they are located. Self-adhesive insulation tape closes gaps in windows and doors and doesn't cost much. Caulk suits smaller cracks and gaps. Expanding foam sealant is better for sealing larger cracks and holes that are protected from sunlight and moisture. Rigid foam works for big cracks, such as plumbing chases. Fiberglass insulation can also be used for those large holes, but it works best when it is wrapped in plastic or stuffed in plastic bags.

Where to check your home for heat loss

There are a number of places around your home that you should check for air leaks:

• Air gaps around the plumbing, wiring, chimneys, ceiling fans, electrical outlets, and switches

• Fireplace valves

• Attic access hatches

• Missing plaster

• Window, door, and baseboard moldings

Go tankless

300 lbs ▬

CO_2 per year

Water heating is the third largest energy expense in your home. It usually accounts for around 13 percent of a household's utility bill. Although most water heaters last 10–15 years, it's best to start shopping for a new one if yours is more than 7 years old. An energy-efficient water boiler will cost a little more than a standard water heater, but in the long run, you'll save money, energy, and carbon with each utility bill. When looking for efficient models, watch for boilers with heavily insulated tanks. You can also increase efficiency by insulating the first six feet of piping— both hot and cold—connected to the water heater.

Tankless heaters are the gold standard of efficiency because they just warm water when it is needed. Researchers have found savings can be up to 30 percent compared with a standard storage water heater. Typically, they provide hot water at a rate of 2–5 gallons per minute. While that's enough to have a good strong shower (a powerful shower flows at about 2.5 gallons per minute), it's probably not sufficient to run the dishwasher and have a shower at the same time. You can overcome this problem by installing two tankless heaters, or reducing your water consumption by purchasing water efficient appliances and low flow showerheads, and by coordinating your water use.

6

Double meals

304 lbs

CO$_2$ per year

It takes less time and energy, and so creates fewer carbon dioxide emissions, to cook a double portion and then quickly reheat it the next day in the microwave. Using the oven just an hour less a week by cooking one double meal could save 304 lbs of CO$_2$ a year. Cooking in bulk and freezing it also saves energy, but cool the meal first, because hot food can raise the temperature of the freezer and spoil other food. Once the dish has cooled, it will freeze more evenly, and will retain more of its natural color and flavor. You can make sure it freezes and thaws quickly and evenly by dividing the food into individual servings before freezing it. Remember to defrost them in the fridge, or at room temperature, and not in the oven for more carbon savings. Don't worry about losing nutritional value: contrary to popular belief, food has about the same amount of nutrients frozen as fresh.

How to freeze your meals properly

- You can freeze a range of foods, including casseroles, cooked poultry, peas, and most vegetables in a sauce. Do not refreeze food after it has defrosted.

- There are also foods that it is often better not to freeze, such as heavily salted foods (because salt lowers the freezing point of water); vegetables with a high water content and delicate cell structure such as broccoli or lettuce; and fruits with a high water content such as watermelon.

- Frozen food doesn't last forever. As a rough guide, stews and sauces can stay fresh for up to six months; fruit and vegetables for about eight months; and cooked poultry for about four months, but raw it lasts about ten months.

Leaky faucets

18 lbs
CO_2 per year

A leaky faucet is a huge waste of water. A tap leaking at a rate of a drop per second can waste more than 6.5 gallons of water per day, or about 2,650 gallons per year. A leaky hot tap not only wastes the same amount of water, it wastes energy too — about 13 percent of your energy bill goes towards heating hot water.

To check if your plumbing system is leaking, locate your water meter and record the reading before going to bed, and again early in the morning, before any water use. If there is a difference between the two readings, you've got a leak. The problem is often a worn-out washer, which doesn't cost much to replace. Remember to note the manufacturer and faucet model before going to the hardware store — the parts aren't usually interchangeable.

A leaking toilet can do even more damage to your water conservation efforts. A bad leak is usually pretty obvious: you would normally be able to see that something was wrong or hear water running. A small leak could be more difficult to identify, although it can still waste 12 gallons of water every hour.

To check for leaks, try adding some food coloring to the holding tank and wait for about 15 minutes. If the color shows up in the bowl without the aid of a flush, it's a leak.

Energy Star

4,920 lbs

CO_2 per year

The Energy Star is a little blue label you can find on a wide range of products and is a good guide on your road to becoming green. It is a logo that shows customers whether or not a product is energy efficient. When it began in the 1990s, it just covered electronics and computers, but today it rates hundreds of products, from air conditioners to cooking appliances, buildings and boilers, fans and furnaces, home and office equipment, so you can make sure all your appliances at home are as eco-friendly as possible.

The very first environmental label was used in Germany, the Blue Angel label, which was introduced in 1978. The Energy Star rating began in the United States, although it now also applies to goods in Europe and Canada. However, many countries, including those in the European Union, have developed their own energy efficiency rating systems as well. So no matter where in the world you're living or traveling, you can make sure that the products and appliances that you're buying are energy efficient.

To display the logo, products must meet specific targets. On average, those that make the grade are about 30 percent more efficient than standard, but the exact figure depends on the type of appliance. For example, approved refrigerators must use high efficiency compressors, improved insulation, and more precise temperature and defrost mechanisms. They must draw 15 percent less power than that which is required by current US government standards, and 40 percent less energy than standard appliances sold in 2001. For a washing machine to qualify for an Energy Star label it must clean clothes using 50 percent less energy than a standard washer, which means it should be using anywhere between 18 and 25 gallons of water per load as opposed to 40 gallons per load in a standard washer.

Environmental labels like the Energy Star label have grown in popularity worldwide with rising concern over climate change. Standards are raised in line with the new technology that comes to the market. Energy Star products saved enough electricity in 2005 to eliminate 23 million cars' worth of greenhouse-gas emissions, according to the Environmental Protection Agency, while saving consumers $12 billion.

How to recognize environmental labels worldwide

Countries all over the world use different energy efficiency rating systems, so if you want to continue to buy eco-friendly products when you are traveling the world, you just have to know which label to look out for.

- The Green Seal is used internationally for products such as paints and coatings, paper, windows and doors, food packaging and household cleaners.

- Ecolabel is the system used in the European Union for electrical appliances, tissue and printing paper, textiles, footwear, mattresses, household cleaners and detergents, soaps and shampoos, soil, floor coverings, paints and varnishes, lubricants, and tourist accommodation.

- The Nordic Swan Ecolabel is used in coutries such as Norway, Sweden, Finland, Iceland, and Denmark, and covers products such as household chemicals, paper products, office machinery, and building materials.

- Ecomark is what you need to look for in Japan for paper, textiles, plastics, electronics, soaps, building products, furniture, paints and packaging, photovoltaic cells, water saving equipment, and wood products.

Full dishwasher

— **100 lbs**

CO_2 per year

Wishes won't wash dishes, as the proverb goes. Luckily dishwashers will, although their convenience consumes gallons of hot water with every load.Most of the energy used to run a dishwasher is used to heat the water, so if you use a more efficient model, you'll use less energy to do the same job. Virtually all dishwashers available today use booster heaters to heat the water above the temperature supplied by your boiler, so even if you lower the water temperature on your aquastat, the thermostat that regulates the water temperature in your house, the dishes will still be blasted with hot water, and come out clean.

When running the dishwasher, you should only need to use the energy efficient settings. Make sure you only run it on a full load—if you only have a few plates that you need to use straight away, it really doesn't take much effort to wash them by hand every now and again. Try not to use the "rinse hold" on your machine for just a few soiled dishes. It uses 3–7 gallons of hot water each time you press it.

Another power saver is to let your dishes air dry. If you don't have an automatic air-dry switch, you can turn off the dishwasher after the final rinse and prop the door open so the dishes will dry faster.

Finally, look for an efficient model, such as those approved by Energy Star (see entry 8), when shopping for a new dishwasher. These use less water and 25 percent less energy than other standard models.

Clogged AC filter

350 lbs

CO_2 per year

Like many luxuries, air conditioners gobble up power. On average, they release 2 metric tons of CO_2 per household every year. When using the AC, remember to replace or clean the filter every 3–6 months. A clean filter will prevent the evaporator coil from collecting dirt and a clogged filter can raise energy consumption by up to 15 percent, by restricting its airflow. Cheap filters aren't really worth the money they save—they rarely need changing because they don't collect much dirt. A more efficient filter will require more frequent maintenance since they remove the dust, dirt, and particulate matter from the air inside.

How to increase the efficiency of your AC

- The best way to lower the carbon emissions of your AC is to only use it when necessary. Curtains and blinds will help keep your house cool during the summer—look for highly reflective fabrics, such as ones sprayed with an aluminum film as these can reflect up to 85 percent of the sun's energy.

- If you have a window unit, check the seal between the unit and the window frame. Moisture can damage this seal, allowing cool air to escape.

- When buying an AC unit, select one with a cooling capacity that matches the size of your room. If it is too small for an area, it will have to run continuously to keep up with cooling needs. If it's too large, it will constantly turn off and on, increasing energy consumption.

- Choose models with a higher Energy Efficiency Rating (EER) which will save carbon emissions and money. Window units have ratings between EER 8.0–12.0 and wall cavity ACs between 8.0–9.5.

Go fluorescent

300 lbs

CO_2 per year

Like fashion, fluorescent light bulbs have come a long way since the 1980s. One reason they have been slow to catch on is they used to be ugly and inconvenient. Not only were they heavy—there were stories of them falling out of their sockets— they were slow to turn on and gave off a cold, bluish light.

Today's bulbs have solved almost all of these problems. They turn on in about 1–3 seconds, radiate an even light in all directions, and are smaller and lighter than their predecessors. They are sold in different spectrums of light (red, green, and blue) depending on the purpose, and can radiate a softer, warmer light. Blue simulates daylight for reading and detail-oriented activities. Red is best for kitchens, bathrooms, and garages. Green produces a warm light like an incandescent bulb. If you're like me, you may have believed that a blue spectrum light was colored blue. It's not—it's still white. It simply says blue spectrum on the packet. If the light bulb is colored blue, red, or green, it's probably meant to be used at parties!

Whatever the spectrum, fluorescent light bulbs are considerably more energy efficient. They work by making a phosphorous coating glow rather than by heating a filament, and they use about 60 percent less electricity to make the same amount of light as an equivalent incandescent bulb. Replacing just three frequently used light bulbs with compact fluorescent bulbs will save about 300 lbs of carbon dioxide per year and the bulbs will last 6–15 times longer than the 1,000 hours of a traditional bulb.

If you've changed over to fluorescents in the past year, you probably haven't given much thought to how to dispose of them once they come to the end of their life span. Compact Fluorescent Lamps (CFLs) last between 6,000–15,000 hours or

5–10 years on average, but once they stop working, they cannot be put in the trash, like regular bulbs. A small amount of mercury is needed to make the bulbs work, about 4–8 milligrams per bulb. This is not significant enough to pose a health risk in your home, but CFLs must be properly disposed of, like batteries, as the bulbs that do end up in landfill release mercury into our air and water which does pose a risk to the environment. There should be a an educational effort made, and a bulb-collection service introduced, to raise awareness of this risk. Many municipal recycling centers or retailers will dispose of the bulbs, although check with the store first, because some shops charge for this service.

Fluorescent bulbs come in different wattages from regular bulbs, and this can take some getting used to. In general, a more expensive CFL bulb is usually an indicator of brightness and lifespan, but it's worth checking the label, or getting familiar with the difference between the wattages of the bulbs so that you don't take home the wrong one.

Comparison guide for CFL and regular bulbs

CFL	Regular bulb
7-watt	40-watt
20-watt	75-watt
26-watt	100-watt

12

Two fridges

30 lbs

CO_2 per year

Fridges use up about 5 percent of the total electricity in your home. Most people just have one, but some households have two, which consumes about an extra 700 kWh a year. If you are one of those people, you might consider buying food in smaller packages or storing some items in the cupboard, if possible. Downsizing to just one fridge will make a big dent in your carbon footprint.

If your refrigerator is more than a decade old, it's likely to be pretty inefficient. Appliances today use much less electricity than older models because energy standards have been tightened in recent years. Today's fridges, particularly the more efficient models, will use less than half the energy of a fridge that was bought 12 years ago.

If you decide to invest in a newer, more efficient fridge, look for the automatic moisture control feature. It means the fridge has been engineered to prevent condensation droplets from forming on the exterior, without the need for any extra warming device to prevent moisture buildup. This is not the same thing as an "anti-sweat" heater, an inefficient device which causes fridges to gobble 5–10 percent more energy than models without this function.

In general, side-by-side refrigerator/freezers use more energy than similarly sized models with the freezer on top or bottom, even if they both carry an eco-friendly label. The government holds the two categories to different standards, allowing side-by-sides to use 10–30 percent more energy. Features like icemakers and water dispensers, while convenient, also consume extra energy and increase your carbon footprint.

Hug your water heater

250 lbs

CO_2 per year

Buying an insulation blanket could be the best money you've never spent. Most water heaters more than five years old are constantly losing heat and wasting energy because they lack internal insulation. Adding a pre-cut jacket or blanket can reduce heat losses by 25–45 percent. If you're not sure whether your heater needs to be wrapped up, touch it. If it feels warm, it's radiating heat and could probably benefit from a blanket.

With electric water heaters, it's not hard to install the insulation and most people are able do it themselves. With gas and oil-fired water heater tanks, it's a little more difficult, and it is best to have a qualified plumbing and heating contractor add the insulation.

Once you've added the insulation, it's best if you keep the water temperature at 130°F or below—which is hot enough to scald—because otherwise the wiring may overheat. You also might consider placing a piece of rigid insulation—a bottom board—under the tank of your electric water heater. This will help prevent heat loss into the floor, saving another 4–9 percent of water heating energy.

Average hot water use

Activity	Amount of water per use
Clothes washing	32 gallons
Showering	20 gallons
Bathing	20 gallons
Automatic dishwashing	12 gallons
Preparing food	5 gallons
Handwashing	4 gallons

Eco-flooring

— **4 lbs**

CO_2 per square foot

With the growing demand for all things green, there are lots of options for outfitting a floor in an environmentally sustainable fashion and they won't necessarily cost the earth—many eco-friendly materials are about the same price as traditional floors.

Options for glass tiles have become increasingly greener as companies integrate recycled light bulbs, ground glass, mirrors, and old car windshields into their ceramic and glass offerings. Using recycled glass tiles instead of regular glass tiles in an average-sized bathroom, for example, could save up to 750 lbs of CO_2 in total. Some green tiles are biodegradable, others may be recycled once they have come to the end of their life, to use as paving for sidewalks and roads.

Another popular material is "natural linoleum." While this might look like regular linoleum, the two materials are different. Regular linoleum is made from a cheaper plastic called polyvinyl chloride, while natural linoleum is made from renewable, biodegradable resources, including linseed oil (made from crushed flaxseed), pine rosin, clay, cork, and limestone with a backing of jute. It comes in many colors and has natural bactericidal properties that inhibit the growth of some microorganisms.

Cork is nothing like the flakey covering you find on bulletin boards—it's solid, sturdy, and comfortable. Made from the bark of cork oak, it is grown primarily in the Mediterranean region of Europe (such as Portugal or Spain) and northern Africa. Harvested by hand about every nine or ten years, the process does not harm the trees since they have ample time to rebuild and only 50 percent of the bark is removed at one time. After the bark is harvested and aged for around 3–6 months, it is cleaned and boiled for production. The rough exterior is cut off and the rest is ground up and mixed in a binder, then molded into blocks and baked. Light, medium, and dark cork colors are achieved by baking the cork at varying temperatures. Cork resists fire, moisture, bacteria, and insects, and it serves as a good insulator for both heat and sound.

Bamboo is another environmentally-friendly alternative to wood. Its expansive root system sends up profuse, rapidly-growing shoots throughout its lifetime, making the grass a highly renewable source. Although it looks and feels like wood, it can grow much more quickly, and can be harvested in a 3–5-year cycle. However, since most bamboo flooring comes from the Southeast Asia, there are high energy and emissions costs related to transporting it.

Eco-friendly flooring options

- Durapalm. Coconut palms are grown throughout much of the world to harvest the nuts, so there is an abundance of this wood.

- Kirei Board. Made from the stalks of the sorghum plant, a cereal crop grown to make molasses, sweetener, biscuits, breads, boiled porridge, beers and other beverages. The stalks used to be considered waste, but now they are heat-pressed together to make a wood-like board.

- Recycled Glass. This is used to make tiles, tables and chairs, and furnishings such as vases. Using recycled glass consumes about 50 percent less energy than using virgin glass.

- The ones to avoid are hardwoods. Species such as merbau, mahogany, and hardwood teak are all slow-growing species. Spiraling demand for merbau has led to concern that this species faces extinction within the next 35 years.

Green power

4,032 lbs

CO$_2$ per year

Going off-grid may sound like the bucolic ideal, but for the vast majority of us, it's not an option. One choice that is more widely available is to power your house with greener energy. The Green Power Network is a good place to start to find out your options. It lists what's available across the United States, but it also has links to what's available internationally. In Europe, for example, Ecotricity is the largest alternative supplier.

You might not have access to a source of renewable energy in your area. If you can't find a supply, you can also choose the green power option from your standard utility company. Your electricity bills will increase slightly, but those raised rates will enable your utility to use a certain amount of their power from wind turbines or a photovoltaic source. You don't directly receive that renewable energy, since it all goes into a kind of melting pot. But the utility promises to use those fees to build new wind farms, solar arrays, or other systems, which helps to move the electricity infrastructure away from the oil economy.

If there are no renewable sources of green power where you live, you can still do your part by purchasing Renewable Energy Certificates (RECs) These are also known as green tags or Tradable Renewable Certificates (TRCs). In effect, they subsidize the renewable power industry, so these companies can invest in wind farms, solar panels, and new research. Renewable energy sources need further investment to develop these new technologies. They might cost more, but there is a positive effect on the climate that everyone shares. One REC buys you the environmental benefit of 1,000 kwh from a green power source. The cost of an REC depends what sort of renewable power sources are available in your area and it varies according to where you live.

Larger homes

3,690 lbs

CO$_2$ per year

In the 1940s, the average house size was 800 square feet. In the 1950s, it was 1,100 square feet. Today in some areas it is over 2,000 square feet. Larger homes use up more resources and energy, for heating for example, than smaller ones. Moving to a home just 500 square feet larger could add up to an extra 3,690 lbs of CO$_2$ a year.

It's not that people need the space, since the average family size is becoming smaller. One reason for the increase, and one that is difficult to counteract, is that people like living in big houses. Another is the influence from real estate developers who are building bigger and bigger houses in the outer suburbs so that people will think it is worth driving the extra distance. As a result people who live in the suburbs drive their cars much more frequently than in the city, and in order to then connect these people to the cities extra highways and power lines need to be built, water, and sewer systems extended, which all add up.

Increase of materials and resources for large homes

Materials/resource	Increase for large home
Copper pipe	5 times more
Land	35 times more
Roadway	15 times more
Water	70 times more
Lumber	4 times more
Heating	5 times more

Ice build-up

200 lbs

CO_2 per year

Refrigerators are one of the most energy intensive appliances in your house. They are on 24 hours a day, and use between 400 and 800 kWh per year. If you can't remember the last time you defrosted your refrigerator, you could be wasting 30 percent more energy than necessary.

How to increase the efficiency of your refridgerator

• Manually defrost your freezer; build-up greater than ¼ of an inch will decrease the energy efficiency of the unit.

• Make sure your refrigerator doors are airtight. Test the seals by closing the door over a piece of paper. If you can pull the paper out easily, the latch may need adjustment, the seal may need replacing, or you might consider buying a new unit.

• Try not to keep your refrigerator or freezer too cold. If you aren't sure whether your thermostat is accurate or not, place an appliance thermometer in a glass of water in the center of the refrigerator and read it after 24 hours. The recommended temperature is between 37° and 40°F. To

check the freezer, place a thermometer between frozen packages and wait a day before checking it. The freezer section should be set to 5°F.

• Cover liquids and seal food stored in the refrigerator, in reusable containers. Uncovered food releases moisture and makes the compressor work harder.

• Regularly throw out old and moldy foods. This may sound obvious, but crusty looking jars and forgotten foods are more common than one might think.

Insulate walls and roofs

2,000 lbs ▬

CO_2 per year

Insulation is your primary defense against heat escaping from your house. Up to 15 percent of heat is lost through the walls and 30 percent via the roof. That said, putting insulation into older homes can be pretty difficult. If you don't have insulation in the cavities in your walls, the best option is to bring in an insulation contractor to blow cellulose or fiberglass into the walls. You can try doing it yourself by drilling the walls and filling the voids with loose cellulose, fiberglass, pellets, or foam, but the equipment is expensive and the job can be difficult.

Adding insulation to an unheated attic is usually a lot easier. A full foot of fiberglass or cellulose is one of the most cost-effective forms of insulation for the attic floor. With new homes, usually the walls and attics are well-insulated, but sometimes the foundations of the house are neglected, which can account for up to 20 percent of total heat loss.

Most forms of insulation pay for themselves within five years or less of installation. Often, there are grants available for these home improvements from your local or federal government.

Cold wash

500 lbs

CO_2 per year

In September 2006, Ariel, a detergent sold in Europe and internationally, launched a campaign to urge consumers to use colder temperatures when they wash their clothes. By washing clothes at 104°F instead of 86°F, the UK wastes 1.6 billion kWh of electricity annually, the company said.

The company cited several studies to back up their claims. In repeated tests, colder water cleans just as effectively, at least for everyday loads. Most modern washing detergents are designed to break down stains in cold water as well as hot. By making the switch, you can lower your carbon footprint significantly. The energy used for hot wash cycles takes up a large proportion of the household's total heating costs. Another way to increase the efficiency and lower the carbon emissions of your washing machine is to only do a wash when you have a full load of laundry.

Washing machines vary greatly in their efficiency. When buying a new one, look for the Energy Star logo (see entry 8) because these models use 40 percent less energy (and release 40 percent less carbon dioxide) than standard machines. Front-loading appliances use less water and energy since their tumbling action is better at circulating water and cleaning than that of the top-loading variety. And, because they don't have a big post in the middle, they also hold more clothes.

Air-conditioning

1,000 lbs

CO_2 per year

Around 85 percent of Japanese homes and two-thirds of homes in the United States have air conditioners. They use about 5 percent of all the electricity produced in the United States, at a cost of over $11 billion to homeowners. As a result, roughly 100 million metric tons of carbon dioxide are released into the air each year—an average of two metric tons for each home with an air conditioner. But you can lower your emissions just by raising the temperature in your house by about two degrees in the summer.

Even on extremely hot days, the need for an air conditioner really depends on the energy efficiency of your home. Window blinds will reflect sunlight and heat, creating cooler interiors. Ceiling fans use less power and release less carbon dioxide than air conditioners. A powerful fan at the top of the house will suck air through the house, creating currents that will draw in cooler air from outside. Trees planted outside provide welcome shade. According to a study done by the Arbor Day Foundation, a single tree provides the same cooling effect as ten room-size air conditioners operating 20 hours a day.

Percentage of buildings with air-conditioning

Country	Work	Home
Japan	100	85
USA	80	65
Europe	27	5

Clothes dryer

1,440 lbs

CO_2 per year

Most people have a collection of energy-guzzling appliances in their home. The dryer is one of the worst offenders for wasting energy. After the refrigerator, it uses a higher percentage of our household energy than any other appliance. In an average family household, dryers account for about 6 percent of the total energy use, and there are many ways that this use of energy could be avoided.

Dryer technology has improved so little in the past few years that Energy Star doesn't even offer a label to distinguish the bad from the better. No matter what kind of dryer you own, it gobbles up greenhouse-gas-emitting energy with each load of wet clothes.

So what are your options? The best option is to line dry your clothes in the sunshine, and take advantage of the world's natural heat source (just remember to keep an eye on the weather). If it's too cold or raining, try hanging them indoors either on a radiator or on a rack. Some racks are made from FSC (Forest Stewardship Council) wood or from wood scraps, so you get extra green points just for buying one.

It can sometimes be hard to find the space to have a line for hanging up your clothes, but if you do have the room, line drying will also stop your clothes from fading as quickly, which is better for those designer wares. If your clothes are drying too slowly this way try hanging them on the line or rack for a little while to remove most of the moisture, then fluff up the fabrics by stuffing them in the dryer for the last few minutes.

A less green but still eco-conscious option is to purchase a gas-fired clothes dryer when you next need a replacement. These models use 60 percent less energy (including the gas) and yet dry clothes 40 percent faster than a standard

dryer. However, gas dryers are a little more difficult to install and must be vented to the outside, so do some research before you make the purchase.

Of course sometimes you do need to use a dryer, but always keep in mind that the most effective way to lessen your carbon footprint is always to reach for those clothes pegs instead.

How to reduce your dryer's energy consumption

- Keep the dryer in a warm part of the house. The machine won't have to work as hard to generate and maintain sufficient heat.

- Dry similar fabrics together. A load of thin, synthetic articles will be done much faster than a mixed load of heavy towels and lightweight sheets.

- Run separate loads consecutively to take advantage of residual heat, and use the Permanent Press setting to complete the tumble cycle with leftover heat.

- Clean the lint filter after every load. Dryers move heated air through wet clothes, evaporating and then venting water vapor outside. If the dryer cannot provide enough heat, or move air sufficiently through the clothes, it takes longer to dry the same load.

- Models that come with humidity sensors shut off the heat when the clothes are dry, which saves energy and money. Look for this option when choosing a replacement.

Sustainable wood

40 lbs
CO_2 per square yard

Hardwood forests store billions of metric tons of carbon, acting like a vast reserve. The sheer scale of these sinks is enormous—it's estimated that the forests in Canada hold more carbon, 12 times more in fact, than the entire world emits annually from fossil fuels.

If you have the choice, it's usually better to avoid hardwood for your flooring or furniture needs as these forests take an extremely long time to grow. Old wood stores more carbon than younger trees, so the older forests lock up more carbon than replacement saplings. However, if you do decide on hardwood, its best to look for FSC-certified products. The Forest Stewardship Council is an international non-profit organization that promotes responsible forest management and approves some of the most popular species of lumber, including white and red oak, cherry, maple, red birch, hickory, teak, rosewood, and cumaru.

To become FSC-certified, logging operations must meet 57 criteria. They must protect local wildlife, use minimal amounts of pesticides, and allow loggers to unionize, among other things. The FSC also tracks the products so they may be traced back to their original sources.

In addition, the FSC also provides certification for paper and printed products, such as envelopes and greeting cards. You can even purchase FSC paper towels and toilet paper, so the planet's forests aren't destroyed by the world's insatiable demand.

Cook with gas

330 lbs

CO_2 per year

The average family uses their oven about 200 times a year. If you have the choice, it's better to cook with gas. Gas ovens typically use more power, but because the power is produced more efficiently, they produce less carbon emissions overall.

That said, not everyone is ready to buy a new oven. Cooking accounts for about 2–5 percent of total household energy use depending on the country; about 5 percent in the European Union, 4 percent in the UK, and 3 percent in the United States. If you don't want to make the switch, here are a number of other cooking tips to cut your carbon emissions.

How to cut your carbon emissions when cooking

- Look into buying a pressure cooker. By building up steam pressure, it cooks at a higher temperature, reducing cooking time. It's estimated that a pressure cooker uses about five percent less energy than a regular oven.

- Use glass or ceramic pans in the oven. You can turn down the temperature by about 25°F and the food cooks as quickly.

- Match the pan to the element size on electric rings. A 6-inch pan on an 8-inch ring will waste over 40 percent of the heat produced.

- Food cooks more quickly and more efficiently in ovens when air can circulate freely. Try to use upper and lower racks to improve airflow if you are cooking more than one dish at a time.

- Stackable steamers cook two or three foods at the same time, saving on energy.

- Use the smallest pan necessary to do the job. Smaller pans require less energy.

Unplug it
800 lbs
CO_2 per year

In the summer of 2001, President George Bush enacted an energy directive that could be an example to households around the world. In July of that year, President Bush, not generally regarded as the greenest of world leaders, ordered the entire federal government to buy only low-standby devices, that is, electronics that use very little electricity (1 watt or less) when they are switched to standby mode.

Most household appliances use considerably more—standby mode can consume 70–80 percent of the total power. In fact, the energy used to keep display clocks lit, and memory chips active accounts for between 5 and 8 percent of total domestic energy consumption.

The simple solution is to buy low-standby devices, or even better, unplug them. However, some people worry about getting an electric shock when pulling out uncooperative plugs. Another concern is the convenience factor—the plug socket is often in a hard to reach place behind the furniture and who wants to scrabble about on your knees, underneath the desk, trying to find the wretched computer cord? These setbacks are very easy to overcome, even among extremely lazy people, myself included. Plug your household appliances into a power bar with an on/off switch, put the power bar in a convenient spot, and flick its switch once you have finished using the device. So always remember when leaving a room to switch off the lights, turn off the the television or stereo, and unplug any charging devices when they are not in use—if a charger still feels warm when it has not been attached to a device, it is still converting energy.

Long showers

340 lbs

CO_2 per year

Showers account for two-thirds of all water heater costs. For many of us, that's money well spent. Standing underneath a steaming hot power shower is one of modern life's most relaxing luxuries. For those of us who want to keep our creature comforts while saving the planet, the low-flow showerheads aren't as bad as they sound. By forcing air into the water flow, they reduce the amount of water used, but still produce a fairly strong spray. These energy efficient showerheads are available in a wide price range and they also range in the volume of gallons of water they release, from 1–2.5 gallons per minute. Some even have a pause button, so you can stop the shower while you soap up. Another way to save on carbon is to have a gravity-fed system, or you could just have a shorter shower. For each minute less, you could save 170 lbs a year. A minute here, a minute there—it all adds up.

How to save water when showering

- A gravity-fed shower uses an average of 10 gallons of water in five minutes, while a power shower can use over 20 gallons in the same amount of time.

- Showering once a day in a power shower would use 4,300 gallons of water more per year than using regular shower.

- Regular showers can be 75 percent cheaper than power showers.

Recycling

3,600 lbs

CO$_2$ per year

Recycling three-quarters of your household waste would reduce your carbon footprint by 3,600 lbs, and it helps the environment in myriad ways. For example, recycling aluminum cans not only saves energy and carbon, but eliminates the need to mine the Bauxite ore used to create the cans. The open-cast Bauxite mining and accompanying deforestation of the Amazon rainforest have long been considered a serious source of environmental concern.

Recycling aluminum uses 95 percent less energy than producing the metal from raw materials, while recycling steel saves 60 percent, newspaper 40 percent, plastics 70 percent, and glass 40 percent of the energy needed to produce it. Glass can be recycled indefinitely as its structure does not deteriorate when reprocessed. It is either reblown into new jars or bottles or used to make materials like glassphalt, made from 30 percent cullet (crushed glass), which is used to lay roads.

With all these obvious and immediate benefits, recycling should really be a bit of a no-brainer. Nevertheless, many people throw out garbage, especially paper products and plastics, that could have a whole new life.

Where to cut down on your household waste

The average household generates more than a metric ton of waste every year. Within this total are many areas where we could easily reduce our consumption so that we are no longer wasting:

- 4 trees worth of paper
- 270 bottles and jars
- 450 metal cans
- 110 lbs of plastic

Wear a sweater

1,000 lbs

CO_2 per year

In the summer of 2007, the UK government came up with a "wear a sweater" campaign. The climate change initiative was the result of some sobering statistics put out by The Energy Savings Trust, the UK government domestic energy watchdog. Heating is the largest energy expense in most homes. It accounts for around two-thirds of annual energy bills, especially in colder climes. Cutting down on heating costs is the single most effective way to save money and reduce your home's contribution to climate change, and you could achieve this by turning your thermostat down by just two degrees in winter. Home heating systems spew out billion of metric tons of CO_2 into the atmosphere each year and about 12 percent of the world's sulfur dioxide and nitrogen oxides.

One of the easiest ways to lower your heating costs is to turn down the thermostat at night and when you are away from home. In most homes, you can save about 2 percent of your heating bill for each degree that you lower the thermostat for at least eight hours each day. Turning down the thermostat from 70°F to 65°F, for example, saves about 10 percent. You can also use a programmable thermostat, so you don't have to remember each day. These can store multiple daily settings (six or more temperature settings a day) that you can manually override without affecting the rest of the daily or weekly program. With the energy savings, you will likely recover the cost of the programmable thermostat in the first year or so, according to a study carried out by the American Council for an Energy Efficient Economy.

Hot water

550 lbs

CO_2 per year

Scalding water is one of the leading causes of accidents involving small children in the home, and rather unnecessary. Unless you are particularly thick-skinned, you probably don't shower with only hot water. Most of us find it far too hot, even for short periods of time. Children certainly do—it takes just 2 seconds for kids to burn with water set at 150°F . Some safety experts recommend families with young kids turn down the aquastat to 125° or 120°F. This is usually located in a metal box connected to the water heater.

If you follow this advice, it will not only improve safety, it will save carbon emissions. Lowering the temperature to 140°F will reduce fuel consumption by 5–10 percent. You may find you can lower the temperature further without sacrificing your creature comforts, especially during the long, hot summer months. Lowering the temperature to 120° or 125°F will save even more energy, and still feels hot enough for most people.

Water temperatures that burn

Temperature of water	Time to cause a bad burn
150°F	2 seconds
140°F	6 seconds
125°F	2 minutes
120°F	10 minutes

LED tree lights

7 lbs

CO_2 per year

If you dream of a green Christmas, or at least a planet where it still snows, switching to LED Christmas lights is an easy change that will cut your carbon output with very little effort. They use 95 percent less energy, and only cost a few dollars more.

This is a new technology that holds great promise. LED lights use between 70–95 percent less energy than regular light bulbs, and are even more efficient than carbon-saving fluorescents. Around the world, they are already used to light up a number of iconic structures, including the CN Tower in Toronto, the Ben Franklin Bridge in Los Angeles, and the London Eye.

Indoors, they are used in shoe showrooms, perfumeries, department stores, and lighting sculptures, such as the world-renowned James Turrell Skyspace at Henry Art Gallery in Seattle. Outside a commercial setting, this technology is affordable for strings of holiday lights, but not quite yet for the rest of our homes. That is expected to change, however, and the cost of LED lights is expected to fall greatly in the next two years so it's worth keeping tabs on this radiant and efficient energy-conserving technology.

Tackling climate change might begin in the home, but it also continues outside and there are plenty of improvements you can make to your garden, or initiatives that will help your local community. Tree planting programs not only help beautify the neighborhood; they also help absorb excess carbon (see entry 37). Or you can check out smart plants, which can be grown indoors and out, and require much less water than lawns (see entry 43).

Some entries in this chapter save more water than carbon dioxide. Water is a precious resource, and in many parts of the world, reservoirs are running low. This precarious situation is expected to worsen in the next few years as one of the consequences of global warming is drought. Water use tends to rise with higher temperatures, exacerbating this problem. Cutting down on your water use doesn't always sizably shrink your carbon footprint, but it is still vitally important for the environment.

Lastly, this chapter addresses a number of ways to generate your own electricity through renewable resources, such as solar, wind, or geothermal energy. For each method, I've evaluated the cost, convenience, and viability. If you only want to invest in one resource, solar water heating is probably your best bet. But since you've got the latest research right here in your hands, it's up to you to decide how you want to act.

Out of Doors

City living

6,174 lbs

CO_2 per year

If you love this planet, then you are better off living in a mega metropolis rather than living in a leafy green home in the rural countryside. Paradoxical as it may seem, studies by John Holtzclaw and others have shown that people who live in compact neighborhoods use less energy and spew less pollution than those who want to live nearer to nature. Why? Living in a city makes it easier to live sustainably without making any special effort. When a neighborhood is spread out, people are forced to drive. When areas are more tightly knit, it becomes more likely that the things we need are close at hand.

When there are 12 homes per acre—equivalent to the density of a single family neighborhood—there are enough customers to entice stores to open up in the area. Public transport becomes cost-effective. People start biking or walking for short trips, instead of always taking the car. When a community hits 40 homes per

acre or more, about the spacing of a row of brownstone houses, everything becomes more efficient. It's easier for the authorities to deliver the mail or pick up the garbage. Water, sewage, electricity, and telephone cables are all shared (the copper used to pipe water and heat to our homes is one of the largest fillers in landfills). When these resources can be used by a number of households, less energy is used to provide them, and that means less CO_2.

Carbon emissions by neighborhood density

	Sprawl	Transit Village	Urban Center	Metro Center
Residential Density (households/ residential acre)	3.2	10	100	200
Land/1,000 households	312 acres	100 acres	10 acres	5 acres
Transit Service (vehicles/hour)	1	27	90	Very high
Shopping (5 stores in ¼ mile)	No homes	25% of homes	All homes	All homes
Pedestrian Amenities	Low	Medium	High	High
Annual CO_2 emissions/capita	14,827 lbs	9,037 lbs	3,863 lbs	1,603 lbs

Patio porch heater

110 lbs

CO_2 per year

A propane patio heater is one of the most inefficient appliances in existence. A single canister with a heat output of 12.5 kW will produce around 71 lbs of CO_2 before it runs out (after approximately 13 hours). This is equivalent to the energy required to produce approximately 5,200 cups of tea (or 400 cups for every hour of operation). Since patio heaters blast energy straight out into the open air, a standard 28 lbs canister of gas will warm an area outside of up to 270 square feet for 12 hours, whereas the same canister used for a gas fire could heat the same area indoors for 10 times longer. Ironically, patio heaters are also more popular during the hottest months of the year: half of all patio heater owners use them mainly during July and August. The pollution spewed out by the heaters even makes cars look green—unlike motor vehicles, they are not fitted with filters to reduce the greenhouse gases they produce, which include carbon dioxide and nitrogen oxides.

"It's difficult to conceive of another item that inflicts more gratuitous damage on the environment than a patio heater," said Tony Juniper, the executive director of Friends of the Earth. "They just blaze energy out into the open air."

Compost

620 lbs ▬

CO_2 per year

Composting your "green" waste (biodegradable, organic waste) has many benefits. It reduces the amount of waste that ends up in your garbage can, ultimately reducing the need for transport vehicles. It gives you fine, homemade compost so you don't need to buy artificial fertilizer. And it keeps some of the most damaging, greenhouse-gas-causing waste from ending up in landfill sites. An average household throwing out one trashcan's worth of waste every week emits about 3,100 lbs of carbon dioxide a year, a figure that you could cut by 20 percent if you compost all kitchen and garden waste. A compost breaks down some items you might not expect it to—paper towels, shredded paper, cardboard, vacuum cleaner bags, biodegradable diapers, and items made from corn plastic. If you are worried about space, you can get a compact compost bin and sprinkle on Bokashi, a Japanese substance which breaks the matter down quickly and should take care of any unpleasant odours.

When you don't compost, and the garbage goes to a regular landfill site, all the organic waste is broken down by microbes to produce a mixture of carbon dioxide and methane. Methane is a global warming accelerator and has 21 times as much "global warming potential" as carbon dioxide. Some landfills offset the excess methane by capturing or flaring off a portion of it, but the remaining gas is released into the atmosphere. If you compost all your food and garden waste, you can save about 11 lbs of methane per year from being emitted from landfill, which is equivalent to just over 220 lbs of carbon dioxide per year. If your whole household composts, you save about 28 lbs of methane a year, equivalent to 617 lbs of carbon dioxide per year. Of course, if you have a green waste recycling program in your neighborhood, chances are that it's making high quality compost from your garden organics. The difference is that it isn't your garden that is reaping the fertile rewards.

Double glazing

1,000 lbs
CO_2 per year

Double glazing is one of the best ways to insulate your house, save energy, and save money on your annual heating bill. Although the number of homes with good double glazing has steadily increased over the years, still only about 40 percent of homes have properly fitted windows. Good window technology can reduce the heat loss of a home by up to two-thirds, so the expense of this investment will pay for itself in the end.

Double glazing works by trapping air between two panes of glass, creating an insulating barrier that reduces heat loss, noise, and condensation. It used to be the most efficient form of window insulation you could buy, until new technologies began coming onto the market about 15 years ago. Two glass panes are still much better than one, but if you are replacing your windows, there are a number of other features that insulate almost four times as well as the best double glazing from 20 years ago.

One of the alternative options is to choose windows where the gap between the glass is filled with a gas that is denser and has a lower conductivity than air, such as argon or carbon dioxide, which is a better insulator and so helps reduce heat loss. Another eco-friendly alternative are windows with a low-emissivity (low-e) coating, where the glass is coated with a silver or tin oxide which allows light to enter the room, and at the same time traps heat inside. These windows are a great option as they are tailored to the climate where they will be used, so northern low-e windows let in lots of light and trap more heat, whereas southern low-e windows do the opposite to keep the room cooler in hot weather. In 2005, Glass for Europe published a study into the carbon saving potential of low-e glass which showed that CO_2 emissions from buildings in the European Union could be cut by 140 million metric tons if the current glazing was replaced by low-e double glazing.

Lastly, when choosing a new window, have a look at the "edge spacers," which are the seals used to hold the panes of glass apart. In the past decade, a number of new materials have come onto the market that aren't expensive to buy, but really make a difference to the efficiency of the windows. Thin-walled steel with a thermal break, silicon foam, and butyl rubber are all environmentally-friendly options that will help you lower your carbon footprint.

How to get the most from double-glazing

- Installing double glazing can be expensive, but it's a competetive market out there, so make sure you get a number of quotes to compare and get the best price.

- Always look for environemental labels when choosing your windows so you can be sure that the whole window (frame and glass) is energy efficient.

- If you're on a budget, fitting secondary glazing could be the answer. It's less expensive than replacement double-glazing and will still save money by cutting heat loss and drafts.

- Another good alternative is to only replace the windows in the rooms where you spend most time and use the most heating.

Rain harvesting

4 lbs

CO_2 per year

Rain harvesters are an excellent way of conserving water. You can go low tech, and buy a rain butt, which is basically a bucket to catch precipitation, with a built in hose to water the garden. Or you can install a more complex system that captures rainwater from roofs via guttering and down-pipes. The water is filtered and then stored for domestic use. Larger systems are usually integrated into the plumbing system, so the filtered water feeds into household appliances, and is used for running the washing machine, flushing the toilet, or even bathing. It's important to leave installation to a licensed plumber, because rainwater and the water from the mains supply must be kept separate so you don't drink anything that hasn't met all the necessary health and safety tests. The more complex systems will likely cost quite a large amount of money to install, but you can save about 50 percent each month on your hydro bill.

Rain harvesters are not the same as grey water. This is the wastewater generated from activities such as washing dishes, laundry, and bathing. Also known as sullage, there's been considerable interest in whether this water can or should be recycled. Most water safety experts will tell you it's more hassle than it's worth, and can end up being a health hazard. If you store this water for more than 24 hours, the bacteria build up, the water darkens, and it soon becomes fetid. Grey water is not clean, and needs to be heavily treated before you use it for anything other than watering the soil. You can use it on flowers or the lawn but don't pour it on any plants you might eat.

Leaf blowers

10 lbs
CO$_2$ per year

Leaf blowers are sold around the world, but there are a number of reasons why these machines don't do the environment any favors. Burning on a combination of oil and gas, they spew out enough fumes to make most cars look like air sanitizers, since they aren't required to have the filters that are standard on car exhaust pipes. The four-stroke engines are generally quieter and cleaner than the two-stroke engines, but they are also heavier and not as popular. In the two-stroke engines, lubricating oil is mixed with gasoline, and at least 25 percent of the unburned fuel spews into the air as exhaust. These models put out as much in hydrocarbon emissions in half an hour as a 1995-model car on a 100-mile trip, according to a study by the California Air Resources Board. In recent years, improvements have made them more efficient, but using the machines for just an hour still sucks down a pint of gas and oil. That's a lot of waste for a job that is almost as easily done by hand, with just a big bag and a garden rake.

Solar heating

3,280 lbs

CO_2 per year

Solar heating of water is one of the most efficient ways for you to utilize green energy. It costs less to install than photovoltaic cells (see entry 45) and is more reliable than wind turbines. If you invest in a more expensive solar heating system, you'll probably save about 50–70 percent of your hot water bill or about one fifth of your home's total energy bill.

Using the sun's energy to heat your hot water through solar panels is an eco-friendly option, but not suitable for every roof. Typically, you need an area of your roof that faces south and a space of about 30 square feet to hold the solar shingles. However, the technology can work without these factors, so it's still worth asking a solar contractor whether or not your house can be retrofitted. If you decide to go ahead with the investment, look for systems with freeze protection, so the pipes can be used in the winter. One of the more expensive components of installation is installing a conduit through which the pipes run from roof to basement. This work can be done independently by a contractor during any home renovation, and it is likely to be cheaper to have this done before hiring the solar contractor to install the system.

Solar water heating tends to get very positive reviews from customers who make the investment and surveys indicate that over 94 percent are satisfied with their systems. And you may be able to write off some of the initial investment—municipal or federal grants or tax rebates are often available to offset the installation costs.

Plant a tree

300 lbs

CO_2 per year

Stressed? Take a look out of your window. If you can see some trees, you're in luck. According to studies by Roger Ulrich, director of the Center for Health Systems and Design at Texas A & M University, results show that looking at a leafy landscape for just five minutes can calm your blood pressure and ease muscle tension.

Trees have many benefits, for us as well as our planet. They soak up carbon, cool the planet, and calm us down. They beautify our homes and increase property values—a street lined with mature oaks is more desirable than a street devoid of greenery. They provide shade for our houses. If planted to act as shade in summer and a windbreak in winter, a tree can make a real difference to your carbon emissions. Make sure you plant a tree that is native to the area, and so suited to the climate and environment (see entry 43).

Lastly, trees help our planet breathe. Made of about 45 percent carbon, when measured by dry biomass, they are excellent sinks for all the excess CO_2 we release. One acre of forest absorbs six metric tons of carbon dioxide and releases four metric tons of oxygen into the atmosphere each year—about enough to meet the needs of 18 people. Planting a single tree won't offset the carbon emissions of a house full of people, but it still absorbs enough carbon to make a sizeable difference.

Day watering

 # 155 lbs

CO_2 per year

Watering the lawn during the day is one of the many ways we waste water in our backyards. Contrary to popular belief, it is not because watering your plants during the midday sun will burn the leaves. The main reason it's a bad idea is the sun will evaporate the water before it has had a chance to sink into the soil and reach the plant roots making it a waste of your time, efforts, and water. The ideal time to water a garden is after the sun sets since you'll lose the least amount of liquid through evaporation.

How to water your plants

- Water plants at the base thoroughly and infrequently, so that water reaches the roots, rather than giving them a light sprinkling more often. Roots will then go down to search for water, making plants stronger.

- Use a rose-head on your watering can so that the water sprinkles out rather than gushes all at once. Water flooded on to the surface will dry to form a hard crust.

- Only water the plants that need it! Some plants, even root vegetables, will survive on very little water. Some, such as potatoes and broad beans, need water when they are filling out and only some, such as lettuces, tomatoes, and marrows need water throughout the season.

- Cut the base off a plastic bottle and bury it upside down next to the plants—water poured in here will then get straight to where it matters, the roots.

- Put a layer of mulch around trees and plants. Chunks of bark, peat moss, or gravel slow down evaporation. This can save up to 750 to 1,500 gallons a month.

Wind turbine

820 lbs

CO_2 per year

Wind turbines work best when there is a strong, steady wind. In cities, where there are buildings and trees creating turbulence and the wind tends to blow in fits and starts from all directions, a wind turbine is not going to give you much eco-friendly bang for your buck. "A wind turbine in a city is like having a car, and driving it over cobblestones," says Sean Whittaker, policy director at the Canadian Wind Energy Association, based in Ottawa. "You can do it, but you won't get a great output."

If you want to take your first few steps toward harnessing wind power, you can probably find a small, relatively cheap one with blades about 3–4 feet in diameter, and an output of 300 watts in a standard hardware store. This would be suitable to charge up a battery, and turbines of this size are sometimes fitted to the sterns of boats at marinas. They are used to power appliances that don't require a lot of power such as radios or lights.

A larger turbine will set you back a bit more, but if you wanted to purchase a more expensive turbine you could get one with blades about 8 feet in diameter, which if placed up high enough can generate about 1,000 watts, or enough to run some of the appliances in your house—a microwave, which is considered a pretty power hungry appliance, requires about 1,000 watts.

If you do decide to invest in a wind turbine for your home, it's a good idea to do some research on "small wind," which is what this alternative power supply is called even when refering to quite large turbines, so that you get the right-sized turbine for your location and your needs.

Community garden

90 lbs

CO_2 per year

Many of today's community gardens were begun during the Second World War and were supported by governments to encourage self-sufficiency during the war effort. Today, community gardens have become more popular with the local food movement, and as a way to become more environmentally-conscious.

Community gardens are ideal in big cities where people may want to plant their own vegetables or flowers, but don't necessarily have enough space of their own. Most are run by non-profit organizations, such as a gardening association, church, the city's parks department, a school, or a university. Usually gardeners are charged a small fee to rent the land. Although some are divided into large plots that could be around 2,500 square feet, the majority are much smaller and are usually between 25 and 400 square feet.

Within this small space, the land can be used for a myriad of purposes. Some gardens are devoted to creating ecological green spaces or habitats, others to furthering education, growing food, or fostering a sense of community within the neighborhood. A community garden can encourage education and civic participation in inner city neighborhoods. For as Cornell University professor Marianne Krasy, founder of the Garden Mosaics movement, asks, "What is a garden, if not an alliance between plants and people, a place where both can thrive?" Since the movement began in 1991, it has expanded to dozens of cities, not just across the United States but also worldwide.

Geothermal heater

5,740 lbs —
CO_2 per year

Geothermal heating systems are among the most efficient, environmentally-friendly heating systems in existance. They operate on a very simple premise: below the frost line, the temperature of the ground stays at approximately 50°F all year round. Since the temperature is constant, the ground can be used as a heat exchanger to warm a house during the winter and cool it in the summer. The heat can also be used to warm the house's hot water. Altogether, these systems can reduce heating and cooling costs by 35–70 percent per household.

These systems work by transfering heat to and from the ground through a long length of plastic tubing. The pipes are filled with a mixture of water and antifreeze that circulates through them. To lay enough piping, you either need a large yard to lay the hundreds, if not thousands of feet of plastic tubing to make the system efficient. Or you can dig down deep to lay vertical coils, but this is more expensive. This environmental solution is not cheap, but there are many financial incentives and grants available to entice people to invest in this carbon-saving technology.

Impact of geothermal heating

The impact of over one million geoexchange systems is equivalent to:

- The elimination of more than 5.8 million metric tons of CO_2 annually.

- Taking almost 1,295,000 cars off the road.

- Planting more than 385 million trees.

- Reducing reliance on imported fuels by 21.5 million barrels of crude oil.

Outdoor lighting

515 lbs

CO_2 per year

Increasing the efficiency of your outdoor lighting can save energy, electricity, and money. It also reduces light pollution, which is better for the wildlife. Making the light source more focused also reduces glare, which can actually make your home more vulnerable to crime. Less glare means more contrast between the lighted and shadowy areas, so there are fewer places for criminals to hide.

There are a number of ways you can make your outdoor lighting more efficient. As well as changing over to fluorescents (see entry 11), one of the most simple ways is to add timers or motion sensors to your lights, so they're not left on constantly. By leaving outdoor lights on all night rather than using a motion sensor, you're adding an extra 515 lbs of CO_2 to your carbon footprint every year.

You could also retrofit your lamps with a shield, so all the light is directed downwards rather than rays shining out into space. By making the existing light more focused, you'll also make it more intense, so your lamps will shine brighter, and you'll need fewer of them. Many lamps can be focused downwards with a simple visor such as a Parshield. These types of visors aren't expensive, but they won't work for every single lamp, so it's worth double checking before you buy.

Outside the home, some places are bringing in tougher legislation demanding shielded lamps and less light pollution. In the United States, two states, New Mexico and Arizona, have banned outdoor lamps that aren't fully focused downwards. Australia and the Czech Republic have brought in similar laws.

Smart plants

86 lbs

CO_2 per year

—

One way to conserve water is to plant foliage that is well-adapted to the natural climate and doesn't need much maintenance. Although there are species of grass that don't need much water or fertilizer, there are also options that are better for the overall environment than a well-kept lawn. Wildflower gardens are ideal since they mainly consist of either indigenous species or plants that are well-suited to the local weather conditions. Getting them growing initially tends to take just as much work as any other garden, but once the wildflowers have begun to flourish, they will provide food and sanctuary for local wildlife like butterflies, songbirds, toads, and other creatures. You can find information on the native and invasive species in your area from natural resource offices, state parks, and invasive plant councils, so you know which ones to favor and which to avoid.

If you live in a drier climate, there are lots of species that need very little water, and they don't all look spindly or desert-like. You don't have to go for cacti, pines, or small hairy succulents with narrow, tiny leaves if these aren't to your taste. Verdant plants and delicate flowers such as juniper, nasturtiums, sage, iris, thyme, crocus, lavender, evening primrose, yucca gloriosa, california poppy, gold dust, and many others all do well in sunny, dry conditions.

Sprinklers

26 lbs
CO_2 per year

Using a sprinkler for just an hour a week can add up to 26 lbs of CO_2 over a year to your carbon footprint. Sprinklers are the most common method people use to water their plants and gardens. While their advantages are cost and convenience, the problem is they tend to over-water plants, usually because they are left on for much longer than they are needed. A sprinkler can use as much water in an hour as a family of four uses in two days.

On average, a typical lawn receives about twice as much water as it actually requires to stay healthy. The excess water is lost to runoff or it flushes out any garden chemicals that have been recently used on the lawn (like fertilizers, pesticides, or weed killers) into the local water system, which then contaminate nearby streams and lakes. When too much water seeps into the soil, it also drenches plant roots and leaches the nutrients away.

The best solution is to use a watering can, as it's really only large lawns that need sprinklers. If you are going to use a sprinkler system though, one solution is to use sprinklers that are buried deep within the soil. By applying water directly to the roots where it can be absorbed, much less is lost to evaporation and run-off.If you have an automatic sprinkler, one way to improve its efficiency is to install a sensor that automatically shuts the water, which can save 15–20 percent of the water you use. These sensors can monitor conditions like soil moisture, rain, freeze, and wind so that plants get the amount of water they need. You can get quite simple sensor systems which shuts off when there has been a rainfall, or there are more sophisticated ones that function like an all-in-one weather station. In general, the installation of these devices on your existing system is simple and highly effective at preventing water waste.

Another trick is to only water lawns when there are signs of water stress. At the first signs of wilting or discoloration, you have about 24 to 48 hours to water before the grass is harmed. On average lawns really only need about an inch of water, which is enough to give them a thorough soaking, while keeping run-off to a minimum. The key is to water the grass infrequently, yet thoroughly. This creates a deep, well-rooted lawn.

How to water your lawn efficiently

- Try not to over-water the grass. Lawns usually only need to be watered every five to seven days in the summer, and every 10-14 days in the winter. A heavy rain eliminates the need for watering for up to two weeks. For most of the year, lawns only need about an inch of water each week.

- Water your lawn in several short sessions rather than one long one so that your lawn is able to absorb more of the moisture.

- Avoid sprinklers that spray a fine mist, since most of it evaporates before it reaches the lawn.

- Make sure you time how long you use a sprinkler or a hose. A garden hose can pour out more than 600 gallons of water in just a few hours.

- Position your sprinkler so that all of the water falls on your lawn, and you're not wasting water on areas like the fence, patio, or sidewalk.

- Check that your sprinkler or hose pipe is properly attached to the water source so that you aren't wasting even more water through leaks.

- To reduce the amount of water you give to your lawn, adjust your lawnmower to cut grass no shorter than three inches. Taller grass encourages deeper roots and shades the soil to reduce moisture loss.

Solar shingles

820 lbs

CO_2 per year

Solar photovoltaics are the most common form of home-generated power. They take a sizeable initial investment but once installed save you money every month on your electricity bill. They can also increase the worth of the house: a power generating feature is increasingly seen as an asset on the housing market.

The cost of a photovoltaic system varies, and some of that cost depends on the look desired. Solar shingles which replace the existing roof covering, create a seamless look. Another option is flexible roofing panels, which are laid on top of the existing roof, so less renovation is necessary. For conservatories, a high-end option is to have glass panels that look dark by day, but switch to flat white glass that radiates LED light at night.

A standard set-up comprises of about five panels measuring 3 by 2 feet that are bolted straight on the roof. This system generates about 1,000 kilowatt hours per year, and is known as 1 kWh system. Depending on the efficiency of your house, a 1 kWh system can provide about 20 percent of the year's total electricity requirements.

Solar systems range in efficiency: the best convert about 30 percent of the sun's rays to electricity and work in low level light. Cheaper, less efficient models don't work as well on overcast days, and might only convert about 12 percent of the sun's energy into electricity. These statistics are a dramatic improvement from the technology just a few years ago. Today's systems generate about twice as much electricity as the latest models did a decade ago. Those figures are expected to continue to improve, especially with help from environmentally-conscious consumers.

Lawn and garden chemicals

730 lbs
CO_2 per year

An emerald-green, even, pristine-looking lawn can be the envy of the neighbors. However, the pesticides, weed killers, and fertilizers likely used to achieve that look can seriously damage the soil and ecosystem underneath. Once these chemicals wash off the grass and soil during heavy rainfall, they can end up in drains, where they are washed into local streams and rivers, poisoning the water and aquatic life. The average homeowner also tends to over-apply these chemicals which can harm the health of the soil, or even cause lawn disease. Outside your garden, they can cause excessive algae growth and eutrophication in the surrounding waterways.

The production of these chemicals releases thousands of metric tons of greenhouse gases. Nitrogen fertilizer is produced under very high pressure and temperatures that range from 750–1,200°F. The fossil fuels burned to reach these temperatures release high levels of greenhouse gases. Producing phosphate fertilizer requires mining of the mineral, which can cause air and dust pollution, and damage water quality, soils, drainage patterns, and wetlands. There is some concern that the radioactive byproducts of phosphate mining (including uranium, radium, and radon gas) can cause increased incidents of cancer among miners and nearby residents.

If you decide to grow your lawn without the use of chemicals, there are lots of eco-friendly solutions for a healthy lawn. Leave grass clippings on the lawn instead of raking them up, they work well in the place of fertilizer; earthworms and other soil organisms keep the soil healthy; and tightly grass is more likely to crowd out weeds.

Green roof

—

2,250 lbs
CO_2 per year

The most obvious reason to install a green roof (a roof that is intentionally covered with vegetation) is to lower the air conditioning and heating costs of your home. However, the real benefits are far greater than that. A green roof lowers dust and smog pollution, dampens noise, and provides a natural habitat for local wildlife. Since the green covering cools the air outside the house, and prevents heat and cool air from escaping, it significantly lowers air conditioning costs in the summer.

Green roofs can be either deciduous or evergreen, depending on the choice of plant. They can be fitted to almost any type of roof with less than a 45 degree pitch. (With a greater slant, there are drainage and maintenance concerns.) Structurally, they are made of four distinct layers. On the bottom is a water and root resistant membrane so the plant roots don't poke through. Then a drainage layer, which funnels away the excess water. Next, the filter layer holds the soil in place and prevents soil from clogging up the drainage layer below. Finally the soil layer is seeded with varieties of simple, durable plants, such as sedums, grasses, and ground coverings.

In general, green roofs cost about twice as much as a regular roof to install. It's also worth asking your subcontractor about maintenance costs. You can choose a low maintenance eco-roof, but like any living, breathing system, it will need care and attention.

Lawn mowers

80 lbs

CO$_2$ per year

Which pollutes more per hour, mowing your lawn on a sunny Saturday morning, or 11 cars roaring down the highway? If your answer was the innocuous-looking lawn mower, you are already an environmentally savvy customer.

The garden equipment used in the US alone spills 17 million gallons of fuel each year—more gasoline than spilled by the Exxon Valdez in the Gulf of Alaska. A typical 3.5 horsepower gas mower, for instance, can emit the same amount of VOCs (pollutants causing smog) in an hour as a new car driven 340 miles. And the mowers that you ride rather than push are far worse: the VOCs they emit are equivalent to 34 cars speeding along the freeway.

The reason that the output of mowers is so much worse is that cars have catalytic converters, devices that filter emissions but generate high levels of heat. Safety advocates worry that the converters could set fire to dry underbrush or grass. Catalytic converters may be introduced in the coming years, although for now, an electric mower is far more efficient. These models are quieter, use only a few dollars worth of electricity a year, and don't require engine tune-ups. Gas mowers aren't required to have the same type of filters as cars and other vehicles, and as a result they produce far more pollution than their size would predict. The best way to mow your lawn, especially if you only have a small lawn, is to use a push mower, which uses no electricity, releases no carbon emissions, and never needs an oil change.

When it comes to transport, there are plenty of ways you can cut carbon. This is an area that is constantly evolving, in terms of better fuels, cleaner cars and greener ways to drive. Eco-driving—or how fuel-efficiently you drive—is about to become part of the UK driving test, but these are useful skills wherever you live. Many of the techniques of eco-driving, such as cruise control, smooth braking, and acceleration, are discussed in the following pages.

Even with these new technological developments, the best thing you can do is leave the car at home. Many cities, including Seattle, London, and Beijing have made heavy investments in public transport recently, as their leaders strive to address the twin problems of pollution and global warming. Paris has invested in a new bicycle system, called the Velib, and other cities around the world are considering whether to follow suit. Bikes are an excellent method of eliminating your car's carbon emissions completely. You save money, often save time, and get fit. And you make a huge difference to your carbon footprint.

PART THREE

On the Road

New fuel

350 lbs

CO_2 per year

Journey to Brazil and you may see a glimpse of the future. The cars look normal—lots of Fords, GMs, Hondas, and Toyotas on the road—but pull into any fuel station, and the question is "ethanol or gas?"

The choice between ethanol or regular gas is one that is increasingly open to all of us. Ethanol is produced by fermenting plant matter, usually corn, but wheat, soybeans, and sugarcane are also used. It can be added to your car's fuel tank at 10 percent ethanol and 90 percent gas (called E10) without any modification. Driving on a purer form of the biofuel is also possible, but the engine needs some adjustments (Brazilians often drive on fuel-flexible engines, which can run on ethanol or gas depending on which is cheaper).

Ethanol was initially touted a godsend by scientists and analysts looking to cut carbon emissions and expand the automobile industry, while replicating Brazil's success. However, there is now some debate over how beneficial this alternative fuel really is. Already, half of the nearly 11 billion bushels of corn—grain that would otherwise be used for food, or farm feed, or any of the other myriad corn-based products—are turned into ethanol each year. Corn soaks up carbon as it grows, but it also takes fertilizers and fossil fuels to harvest and process it. And once distilled, the fuel has to be trucked to the filling stations: it can't be funneled through existing pipelines as it corrodes the iron inside.

That's why alternative-fuel researchers are prospecting for more alternatives, ones that don't rely on food-crops or heavy subsidies. One solution is to produce ethanol from woodchips, sawdust, or paper pulp. Once these are broken down, they produce something called cellulosic ethanol, which packs more energy per tankful. The problem with this is that these do of course come from trees, and so poses a potential threat to forested landscape, but it can also be produced from many other types of matter: grasses, ground-up paper sludge, municipal waste, even sewage. Currently, the substance with the most potential is a prairie crop called switchgrass. Unlike corn, it's easy on the soil, grows like a weed, requires very little fertilizer and not much water, and protects against soil erosion. All these factors are big pluses, but the fuel still needs more research and development.

While cellulosic ethanol isn't widely available, ethanol is gaining acceptance as a green alterative. Corn ethanol releases about 30 percent less CO_2 than a gas-run car, according to a study by Natural Resources Canada, which does add up over the year. More importantly, it moves the economy away from oil and its infrastructure, and boosts an industry poised to turn straw into green gold.

Environmental pros and cons of ethanol

- According to a study by the Argonne National Laboratory, vehicles that use ethanol actually help offset fossil fuels' greenhouse gas emissions by 35–46 percent.

- Corn ethanol encourages the use of highly erodible lands, drives up the price of corn, and so increases food prices, and corn that is grown for oil is too oily to be used as food.

- Ethanol reduces particulate emissions, especially fine particulates that pose a health threat to children, senior citizens, and those with respiratory ailments. The US ethanol industry is the fastest growing energy industry in the world.

Bike it

— **11,560 lbs**

CO_2 per year

Biking is one of the most efficient modes of transportation in cities. For trips under 3 miles it is usually the fastest mode of travel, according to a Canadian government study. On average, bicyclists cover nearly 2 miles in 15 minutes, so bikes usually make the most sense for a busy schedule—and they keep you fit. And of course their carbon emissions are zero, so they're good for the environment too.

For these reasons, a number of cities worldwide are embracing schemes to encourage their citizens to start biking. One of the most successful has been in Paris, which began on July 15, 2007, the day after Bastille Day. Thousands of bikes have been distributed throughout the city, along with rental stands for easy hire. The bikes cost next to nothing to rent—they are free for the first 30 minutes, and then riders pay a little more than a dollar for the next half an hour, although if the bike is returned to a stand and re-checked out, they are free once again.

The program is still in its early days, but walk around Paris, and on almost every road, you see cyclists who have been won over by the convenience and advantages of the scheme. "It's great," says Simon Jackson, a 28-year-old Parisian who started bike riding when the program launched. "Lots of people started biking simply because the bikes are so easy to use. You suddenly realize that biking is not only convenient, and quick, but also a lot of fun."

Take the subway

2,000 lbs

CO_2 per year

Switch from driving to public transport for just one day and you'll make an immediate difference. A single person can save about 20 lbs of CO_2 per day, according to a study carried out by the American Public Transport Association. That adds up to about 2 metric tons per year.

A full subway train can remove more than 2,000 vehicles from the road. Because of its efficiency, many governments are actively pursuing public transport as the only way to lower pollution, traffic, and greenhouse gases. London has introduced an electronic ticket system that speeds people in and out of tube stations, and has cut prices. Beijing will put an extra 3,000 buses on the road by 2010, and increase the number of subway lines from five to twelve.

Benefits of public transport

- Public transport lowers pollution as it produces 95 percent less carbon monoxide, about 50 percent less carbon dioxide, and 50 percent less nitrogen oxides per mile compared to cars.

- Public transport increases property values. Homes that are located near public transport and so linked to local amenites are often worth considerably more (studies show house prices increase by 13–45 percent depending on the city and neighborhood).

- Public transport is also safer, according to the United States National Safety Council. Each mile traveled by car yields 25 times more fatal accidents compared to the same distance traveled on public transport. Injury rates are also lower per mile. Be kind to yourself and the environment: take public transport.

Ditch the car

— 10,400 lbs

CO_2 per year

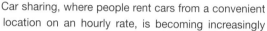

Car sharing, where people rent cars from a convenient location on an hourly rate, is becoming increasingly popular. It's a bit like a regular rental service, but there are key differences. Customers pay according to hourly rates that can vary by duration of usage and time of day the car is rented. Generally there is a membership fee to join a service, and then members can reserve the time they will need the car by phone or over the internet. Many car-sharing services use smart cards to unlock the doors, and track the driver's usage. When the trip is finished, the customer returns the car to the same pickup spot, and the digital card calculates the charges, which are charged to the user's debit or credit card.

Car sharing services tend to be scattered throughout the city in places that are easy to reach on foot, such as near grocery stores or college campuses. The concept seems to be taking hold; there are now more than a dozen different car sharing companies across the United States, and some rental car companies have also started to offer hourly rates.

Driving aggressively

2,750 lbs

CO_2 per year

If you drive like you've got something to prove, you not only waste fuel and your own money, but you jack up your carbon emissions and harm the planet needlessly. Aggressive drivers accelerate and brake quickly, which wears on the engine, and increases the amount of carbon you emit per mile.

Anyone can reduce their emissions if they adopt a few simple techniques. A good rule of thumb is to try and keep the engine below 2,500 rpm (gas) or 2,000 rpm (diesel). Try to accelerate and break smoothly and anticipate the road conditions. Don't rev the engine; it irritates people and releases carbon dioxide unnecessarily. You don't need to drive slower than everyone else, but you should try to drive at a constant speed. The trick is to use the car's momentum to propel you forward. One second of flooring the gas pedal can produce as much carbon monoxide as a full half hour of normal driving. Carbon monoxide is a greenhouse gas, and it is also one of the substances that make up smog.

How to cut carbon emissions when driving

- Try to avoid driving in lower gears where possible as higher gears are more fuel efficient.

- Move into fifth gear at speeds between 45 and 55 mph.

- Try to plan your journeys ahead of time as much as possible to avoid congestion and getting lost, so have your route planned, and check the travel bulletins for any problem areas.

- Reduce wind resistance. An unused luggage rack decreases efficiency by nearly 2 mpg (6 percent) along the freeway.

Carpool

1,600 lbs
CO_2 per year

Carpooling is a growing trend, but still only a small minority of commuters make use of carpools and most don't even consider it. The sad fact is that in many areas 80 percent of people still drive to work alone when sharing a ride with someone just two days a week could reduce their carbon emissions by 1,600 lbs a year.

Which is why you can make a difference by carpooling. If you're looking for a ride or have one to share, there are great websites for connecting passengers and cars across the world, and a number of these services are free. They connect commuters and cars according to where they live and where they are going, with data tailored to your specific area. You just have to search on-line according to where you live and your final destination. Some companies have their own carpooling programs and there are government-funded programs as well.

Carpooling isn't just for getting to work either; consider carpooling to get your children to school and after-school activities. So if you have kids, and there isn't a convenient transportation service, why not set up a carpool? Each parent takes a turn at bringing the children to school on their day and gets a number of free mornings in return. With a little organization carpooling can save time and help our quickly-warming planet.

Idling

240 lbs

CO_2 per year

Idling your car for just five minutes a day really does have an impact. Far too often you'll come across someone waiting outside a store in their car for the passenger to return. The car, often an SUV, is left with the engine running, and the driver seems completely oblivious to the pollution he or she is pumping out into the world. Nor do they notice the growing irritation of pedestrians passing by who dislike having to breathe in their exhaust

Please don't idle your car. Even if it's just for a few minutes, shut it down. If you're stuck in a traffic jam, and you expect to be there for more than a minute or two, switch the engine off. Some people believe that it takes more energy to start a car, and so idling for a few minutes just about balances this out. This is merely a myth: the energy required to start your car is equivalent to about 10 seconds of driving. Modern cars don't need their engines to be warmed for five minutes to work efficiently.

The weather shouldn't make a difference either—today's vehicles are designed so you can just start it up and drive away. Diesel engines can be a little rough starting, but the best way to overcome this problem is to add cold-weather treatment or an anti-gel additive to your fuel. Warming the engine while parked is bad for the engine, whether diesel or gas, not to mention the environment. It causes rapid engine wear, especially in cold weather, and it wastes fuel and releases unnecessary carbon dioxide into the atmosphere.

Large car

4,400 lbs
CO_2 per year

Take a close look at fuel efficiency and the size of your vehicle when you are making your next purchase—if you want to help the planet, size matters. A smaller car with a smaller engine will produce less CO_2 than the gas-guzzling 4x4. There's plenty of information available for almost every model of car, identifying the best models and the worst offendors.

This may seem like an obvious point, but there is a great deal of difference in the carbon emissions of cars. A six-speed convertible with a powerful torque and a larger engine can release five times the greenhouse gases as a small hatchback that has traveled the same distance. The rule of thumb is that hatchbacks are better than sedans, which are better than station wagons, which are greener than SUVs, but it does depend on the type of car, the model, and the efficiency of the engine.

Carbon emissions for different car models

Car Model	CO_2 emissions
Ferrari, Model 599	1.74 lbs/mile
SUV	0.71—1.38 lbs/mile
Minivan	0.68—0.89 lbs/mile
Chrysler Voyager	0.81 lbs/mile
Honda Accord	0.79 lbs/mile
SUV hybrid	0.66 lbs/mile
Ford Fiesta	0.5 lbs/mile
Hatchback	0.53—0.68 lbs/mile
Hybrid	0.37 lbs/mile
Toyota Yaris	0.35 lbs/mile

Fewer short trips

2,300 lbs

CO_2 per year

You could decrease your yearly carbon emissions by this much just by cutting the number of short trips you make by one fifth. Here's a quick eco-puzzle. Imagine you have a car, and on Monday you take four trips, 5 miles each. On Tuesday, you visit a friend who lives 10 miles away. You stay the whole day, so you just use your car twice—for the trip there and back. Assuming all other things are equal, did your car emit the same amount of carbon dioxide on both days, or did you emit more on one day than the other?

On first glance, this problem looks easy. A quick bit of addition reveals that you drove 20 miles on both days. So assuming the amount of carbon dioxide per mile is the same, you should emit the same greenhouse gas emissions on Monday and Tuesday, right? Actually, no. A cold engine uses almost twice as much fuel and catalytic converters can take 5 miles to become properly effective. So if you combine your trips, you'll save carbon even when you would be traveling the same distance. All it takes is a bit of planning in your day to merge all your little trips into one. And remember, if it really is only a short way, you could consider biking or walking instead.

The other advantage of combining all you short trips into one is that you won't have to travel the same distance since you're only making one trip back home. So you save time, money, gas, and carbon. Not bad for a day's work.

Jetsetting

 # 3,600 lbs

CO_2 per year

Almost all means of travel result in some greenhouse gas emissions, but there is no bigger culprit than travel by air. Around the world, air travel is probably responsible for about 3 percent of all carbon emissions. Flying also emits nitrogen oxides which trap heat, and huge quantities of water vapor, which has also been linked to global warming, although how this happens is not yet completely clear. When you go on vacation, 90 percent of the emissions that you release during this time will occur in the air, according to recent research from George Washington University. A single long-haul return flight can produce far more carbon dioxide per passenger than your car will throughout the whole of the rest of the year. Taking just two long haul flights a year could add 3,600 lbs to your carbon footprint.

Moreover, air travel is on the rise, with the growth of air traffic standing at 5 percent a year. Fortunately, planes are also getting more efficient. On average passenger airline fuel efficiency improved by about one third between 2000 and 2006. Further improvements could be made if pilots changed the way they fly. Abrupt drops in altitude waste fuel, so some experts are advocating a policy of "continuous descent" until the plane reaches the runway.

Should you decide to go on vacation abroad, it is better for the environment if you pick a route that is as direct as possible, rather than one with several layovers. A more round-about trip is not only more stressful and time-consuming for you, it also burns through more fossil fuels, as take-off and landing require more fuel than cruising. So a journey broken into more than one flight will release unnecessary excess carbon which really does add up in the long term. For example, the International Air Transport Association estimates it will save 84,800 metric tons of CO_2 annually by negotiating a new route from China to Europe, which has shaved off 30 minutes of flying time. Of course, the best way to reduce plane emissions is to not to fly at all, and enjoy the best of what's in your area if you're taking a vacation. If you are going to go abroad, taking one longer vacation will have a lower impact than going on several short trips if you are flying each time. Or try and use alternatives to flying if possible such as high speed rail or even ferries. If you're a regular business traveler, consider whether you could perhaps use videoconferences rather than flying to business meetings.

Typical carbon emissions for flights

Type of flight	Distance	Hours	CO₂/mile	Total CO₂ lbs per person
Short haul	300 miles	1.5 hours	64 lbs/mile	450 lbs
Medium haul	1,200 miles	4 hours	45 lbs/mile	1,800 lbs
Long haul	3,000 miles +	7 hours +	39 lbs/mile	4,400 lbs

Use cruise control

600 lbs

CO_2 per year

In the summer of 2007, the power company British Petroleum launched a green driving test. The point was to see how economically and efficiently motorists could drive. Journalists, celebrities, and members of the public were invited to the testing grounds in Millbrook, England to test their environmentally-friendly colors.

Each of the participants was given a quarter gallon of gas and a Ford S-Max. The gas had been specially created to improve fuel consumption by cutting down on carbon deposits, meaning more energy could be spent propelling the car. With this they had to make it around an 8-mile course, complete with hills, sweeping bends, and valleys.

The results, many of which are posted on the web, make for hilarious reading. Most of the participants turned out to be pretty clueless about how to lower their carbon emissions while driving. There are several accounts of journalists who stalled and sputtered while driving up gentle slopes, while BP engineers stood by (and presumably tried not to smile). One tip to take away—use cruise control. The cruise function won't make a difference to how the engine performs, but it will stop you from accelerating to overtake the car in front. Rapid acceleration causes traffic jams—far more jams are caused by drivers accelerating and then breaking quickly than by other factors such as accidents—and it burns up fuel and pumps out pollution, including greenhouse gases.

Clean and maintain car

200 lbs ▬

CO_2 per year

The number of miles you squeeze from a gallon of gas depends on many things, including the size of your car and how you maintain it. If you keep your car in good condition, you'll not only save on fuel and repair costs, you'll pump fewer greenhouse gases into the atmosphere.

How to maintain your car's efficiency

- Clear the junk out of your trunk. Golf clubs, bowling balls, and other heavy items belong in the house or garage, not in your car. For every 100 lbs of extra weight in your vehicle, your gas mileage will drop by about 2–3 percent.

- Check your tire pressure each month, in the morning when the tires are cold. Under-inflated tires wear down more quickly and they can also lower your car's gas mileage by up to 15 percent.

- Fixing a car that is out of tune or has failed an emissions test can boost gas mileage by about 4 percent.

- Keep a close eye on your engine's air filter and have it checked at each oil change. When the engine air filter is clogged with dirt, dust, or bugs, your engine has to work harder. Replacing a clogged air filter can improve your gas mileage by as much as 10 percent.

- Improve gas mileage by 1–2 percent by using the manufacturer's recommended grade of motor oil. Opt for oil with the words "energy conserving" on the API performance label—it contains friction-reducing additives.

Speeding

140 lbs

CO_2 per year

Of course, the simplest way to save carbon when on the road is to use more eco-friendly forms of transportation such as a bikes, trains, or buses rather than drive your own car. But when you do need to drive, there are driving practices that will cut your carbon emissions as well as helping you to save money.

Vehicle emissions are at their lowest when traveling between 40 and 60 mph. Once you push it past 60 mph, you start emitting more CO_2 with every mile you drive. Revving the engine doesn't help your carbon footprint either—try to accelerate and brake smoothly to keep emissions to a minimum. "If one person adopts green driving techniques it's not going to halt the rise in sea levels," explains Bob Saner, independent consultant at the UK-non-profit organization Energy Saving Trust. "But if everybody adopts the techniques you may see vehicle CO_2 emissions drop by around 10 percent. It's not a total solution but the beauty is that it's a no-cost solution and can be done immediately." Reducing your speed from 65 to 55 mph may increase your fuel efficiency by as much as 15 percent.

New tires

460 lbs ▬

CO_2 per year

Low resistance tires are a simple, cheap change you can make to your car that will save on fuel usage and carbon emissions. They aren't much more expensive than regular tires but they save energy by minimizing the resistance between the tire and road.

If your first concern is about safety, there isn't any reason to worry. Some people don't like the handle of these tires, since they roll more easily on the road, and don't grip as well on sharp turns or hard driving. But since you've read the entry on green driving, you've weaned yourself off the pedal-to-the-metal, tight-turns type of driving, haven't you?

If you decide to go ahead with low rolling resistance (LRR) tires, you could make about a 4 percent difference to your fuel economy. Most major tire manufacturers now produce these models, so they aren't difficult to find and buy. The Green Seal label offers a guide to which LRR models optimize performance and efficiency, and gives a number of recommendations depending on your needs.

Walking bus

3,600 lbs

CO_2 per year

At first glance, it seems like a contradiction—you're either walking or on the bus, not both. But take a closer look, and the walking bus makes perfect sense. Kids walk to school on designated bus routes, accompanied by at least two adults. The first acts like the "driver" and sets the course for the children behind. The "conductor" brings up the rear. There's even a timetable that matches school hours and bus stops to pick up passengers. Walking buses are starting to catch on worldwide; there are reports of communities and towns in the UK, US, Canada, New Zealand, and others trying out this new mode of transport.

The European Union's 2007 White Paper on Nutrition, Overweight and Obesity recommended more walking bus schemes to teach kids the "life skills necessary to maintain a healthy lifestyle." When questioned, kids say they like it too—a survey of kids and their parents at Scoil an Spioraid Naoimh, an elementary school in Country Meath, Ireland found the majority were in favor, especially since they could talk to their friends on the way. The initiative reduced traffic congestion around the school's gates and raised community spirit by involving local residents. Since it first started in June 2004, a number of other schools in the area have begun walking buses of their own.

Air conditioner

1,150 lbs

CO_2 per year

Stepping into a hot car on a sticky day seems justification enough to turn on the air conditioner. But if you cut down your AC use by two thirds you could save 1,150 lbs a year. It's simply not true that the drag on the car from open windows balances out the extra fuel consumption from the AC. Tests have shown that speeding down the highway at 65 mph with all the windows open reduces your fuel consumption by 2 to 3 percent, while the AC reduced efficiency by 15 percent. You do the math.

How to reduce your AC use

- Air conditioners are gas guzzlers. They increase your fuel consumption by 5 to 20 percent, depending on the car and the driving conditions. There are times when you may feel you just can't live without them, but there are also a number of things you can do to keep their use to a minimum.

- Park your car in the shade. Or if there isn't any space, try using sunshades or car covers to screen your car and stop it absorbing so much heat. Leave the windows open about three quarters of an inch to flush out the hot air.

- Consider having your windows tinted with solar control film.

- When you next buy a car, choose one with tinted windows and a light-colored exterior to reduce the need for AC.

- The AC reduces fuel economy most during acceleration. Wait to turn on your air conditioner until you have reached cruising speed.

- If you do need to use the AC, once the car has cooled to a comfortable level, turn the AC to a warmer setting at a high fan speed.

Hybrid car

5,100 lbs

CO_2 per year

Imagine driving a car that is so efficient and so quiet that you can't tell whether or not the engine is running. That is the experience of driving a hybrid. They work by capturing the energy that is normally lost as heat when the car breaks and using it to charge the battery. Because the energy is recycled, there is less wear and tear on the engine and the breaks. On average, they are about 40 percent more fuel efficient than other cars, which means about 40 percent less CO_2 per gallon of gas with every mile you drive. They still feel just like a regular car to drive in terms of power, and contrary to popular belief, you don't have to worry about changing the battery of a hybrid, since most manufacturers promise it will last the car's lifetime.

Hybrids aren't the perfect solution, as you still release CO_2 into the atmosphere, but they do make a difference. There is still some discussion about what a hybrid represents. Are they the greenest way of doing a polluting activity? Or are hybrids a way of investing in a superior, more environmentally friendly activity? The difference may sound insignificant, but will probably determine how you feel about SUV hybrids. Some people view these as the best of both worlds—a way to own an SUV without having to feel guilty about its carbon footprint. Others wonder whether a product of green technology that puts out the same emissions as a regular car should really be considered all that environmentally friendly.

Currently, hybrids occupy a small percentage of the car market. That is expected to change as new models come into production, consumers become more environmentally conscious, and the cost goes down. At the moment, hybrids are about 15-20 percent pricier than regular cars, but remember to factor in the gas money you save on gas. If you drive 12,400 miles per year—which is about average—you'll recover about half of up front costs in about four years.

Diesel

3,500 lbs

CO$_2$ per year

Diesel cars used to have reputation as dirty vehicles. They had better mileage and released less carbon dioxide per mile, but they also released more nitrogen oxides, particulate matter, and sulfur dioxide. Particulate matter is one of the factors likely to be the cause of higher asthma rates in cities.

However, diesel fuel has had an extreme makeover in the last couple of years. First, ultra-low sulfur diesel was introduced in Europe in 2005 and the United States in 2006. In addition, a new generation of clean burning engines will hit the market beginning in 2008.

With these changes, diesel has become a fuel that burns as cleanly as regular gas, but gets about 30 percent more mileage, says John Bennett, executive director of the non-profit organization Climate for Change. New car buyers might even prefer them to a hybrid vehicle since they release less carbon dioxide when traveling long distances, Bennett says."If you're doing a lot of city driving, a hybrid car is still the best. But if do a lot of highway driving, you should seriously consider going for diesel." And with a diesel engine, you can switch to biodiesel fuel, which has lower carbon emissions than even clean diesel.

Biodiesel

3,900 lbs

CO_2 per year

Imagine a fuel that burned cleanly, but with a powerful kick, and which could be made of almost anything: used grease from restaurant cooking containers, animal fat, or canola oil. Actually, such a fuel already exists. It's just not widely used—yet. Biodiesel is primarily made from vegetable, sunflower, safflower, soybean, palm, cottonseed, rapeseed, or peanut (Demirbas) oil. Once it is refined, it burns substantially cleaner than petroleum-based fuel, releasing 78 percent less carbon dioxide, according to a joint study by the US Departments of Energy and Agriculture. It is also better for human health. Several studies show that the exhaust of biodiesel vehicles has less of the hydrocarbon compounds and other toxins (such as nitrited PAH compounds) that have been linked to cancer.

Biodiesel can be used in any diesel engine when it is blended with gas. Most engines can take 20 percent biodiesel without any modification. However, the warranty usually only covers up to a 5 percent blend since there can be maintenance issues at higher percentages.

Since biodiesel is primarily made from crops which absorb carbon, it is considered carbon neutral. To reduce emissions, a number of public buses and taxis are switching over to a biodiesel blend. San Francisco opened its first biofuel refueling station in April 2007, and there are plans to convert all the buses over by the end of the year. In Graz, Austria, many of the taxis run on biodiesel blends. In Canada, the Port of Vancouver switched to this biofuel in 2006, and the change caused greenhouse-gas emissions to fall by 30 percent. If there are public or school buses in your neighborhood that haven't made the switch, it's worth raising the issue with the appropriate authorities. A lack of awareness is one of the main roadblocks to widespread use.

With a diesel car, it's easy to make the switch, but the main issue often is where to buy the biofuel. There are detailed instructions on how to make your own biodiesel on the Internet, but this is not really recommended as it can be hazardous. Biodiesel is available at selected locations; it can be hard to find, but there are websites that provide lists of participating distributors.

Although there is some confusion, biodiesel is not the same as raw vegetable oil. Straight vegetable oil can be used as a biofuel in a diesel engine, but the engine needs to be modified so it can handle this thick, viscous fuel. If you pour vegetable oil into your engine without these adjustments, you won't save the planet, and are likely to damage your engine.

Why use biodiesel?

- Biodiesel produces much fewer pollutants than regular diesel. In total it produces 90 percent fewer toxins, including sulfur, carbon monoxide, particulate matter, and hydrocarbons. It also releases 78 percent less carbon dioxide than burning gasoline.

- It has the highest energy balance of any alternative fuel, and when blended with conventional diesel it can be used in any diesel engine with little or no modification to the engine or fuel system, unlike other alternative fuels.

- Biodiesel can also benefit your car. It enhances fuel lubricity, which can increase the life of heavy-duty engines, and acts as a solvent which cleans engine systems.

- It can be produced from almost anything, including vegetable oils, animal fat, yellow grease, restaurant grease, lard, tallow, or even sewage. A New Zealand company has produced samples of the fuel from sewage ponds and is now planning to increase production.

Your place of work has a huge impact on global warming. The heating, cooling and powering of office space is responsible for almost 40 percent of carbon dioxide emissions in the US and gobbles up more than 70 percent of total electricity usage. These figures have risen continuously in the last 30 years, and are expected to continue to rise, unless we change our behavior.

You might think your actions don't make much difference, but according to *Time* magazine, a simple office worker can use a quarter ton of materials in a year, including 10,000 pieces of paper. If your office switches over to fluorescent light bulbs, it will save 298,000 lbs of CO_2 per year. This is six times the carbon the average North American releases per year, and an entire year s worth of carbon for 16 Europeans (In total Americans emit more than double the greenhouse gases compared to Europeans).

Obviously, at work there are some decisions we can't control. Often it's an office manager who decides whether or not to purchase recycled paper or the exact temperature the office thermostat is set to. Whatever your role, it's worth bringing up these issues or even suggesting an office wide campaign. It only takes one person to suggest a workable environmental strategy. Good ideas, especially those that save energy and money, are usually those that quickly take hold.

PART FOUR

At Work

Recycle cartridges

— **38 lbs**

CO_2 per year

If you want to cut down on some of the plastic you use, recycling your printer cartridges is a good place to start. In North America alone, over 350 million cartridges are discarded each year, while in Europe 240 million cartridges a year. Currently, only about one third of all printer cartridges are recycled while the rest end up in landfills, where it can take hundreds of years for them to decompose. Creating new cartridges requires a great deal of oil—it can take 2 pints of oil to make an inkjet cartridge, and about 8 pints of oil to make a laser cartridge. The amount of oil you could save by recycling your cartridges could reduce your carbon footprint by 38 lbs of CO_2. There are other factors that could affect your carbon saving, such as the amount of plastic you're saving from landfill, but research into this is not yet final.

If you're unsure of what to do with your empties, you can probably take them back to the store where you first purchased the cartridge. It's worth phoning and checking whether they participate in a recycling program. There are stores that do take back empty cartridges, and some will even pay for certain brands while others take back cartridges and refill them. You can either have it done while you wait, or buy pre-filled refills for the more popular brands. The cost is up to 50 percent cheaper, with bigger savings on the larger-sized refills. There are also plenty of charities that you can send your empty cartridges to, as they raise money by refilling and reselling them, so you'll be doing a double good deed.

Telecommute

6,000 lbs —

CO_2 per year

One of the most pervasive and significant changes brought about by digital technology is the idea of a new workplace. Thanks to such devices as laptops hooked up to wireless internet, many non-manual jobs can now be done almost anywhere—at home, in a car, or even on a park bench.

These changes have brought about the growth of telecommuting, the trend of people working outside the office for at least one day per week. Although an exact count is difficult, the number of telecommuting workers is estimated between 28 and 32 million in the United States, while around 3 million people in the UK are home-based or regularly work from home. Many choose to work away from the office to cut down on travel time or spend more time with family. The advantages are more flexibility, improved productivity, and greater employee satisfaction. Since it cuts out the commute, many governments have embraced telecommuting as a way to tackle global warming.

Benefits of telecommuting

- Save energy. By telecommuting you're cutting down on your driving which means lower fuel consumption.

- Save money. Avoid the costs associated with commuting, whether it's the gas for your car or the fare for public transport.

- Save time. The average commute takes about an hour, so you're gaining extra time in the mornings and evenings. And you will have more flexibility and control over your schedule.

Junk mail

99 lbs

CO_2 per year

Junk mail is a global scourge, an inconvenience, and a stupendous waste of paper that fills up your mail box and takes up your time with catalogues you will never order from, credit cards you will never apply for, and a myriad other pointless letters and forms. On average, Americans receive 11 pieces of unsolicited mail every week, which adds up to about 26 lbs of junk mail each, every year. Other countries don't seem to do any better—each year the British population receive about 9 lbs per person, and the French receive about 22 lbs per person. Globally, the problem costs the planet 100 million trees each year.

Wherever you live, there are certain steps you can take to cease this flow of unwanted paper. Tell the people who sell your information on that you want to opt out of their mailing lists. Marketing companies collect personal information from people all over the world. If you don't want to be part of their ever-expanding database, you can get in touch with them and ask them to withdraw your name and address. Or if there's a particular company that's sending you unwanted stuff, contact them directly. Alternatively you could provide an e-mail address instead of your mailing address and you can continue to receive the information while still reducing unnecessary carbon emissions.

Reusable container

16 lbs

CO_2 per year

People often buy bottled water or other bottled drinks when they're out during the day because they don't want to carry a reusable bottle around with them all the time. They don't have the space for one in their bag, they don't want the extra weight, and they don't want it to leak all over the rest of their belongings.

The trouble is most people also don't bother to recycle all these plastic bottles afterward, so all that plastic ends up in landfill sites. In reality it would be very little trouble to simply buy a reusable bottle, or thermos, or even just reuse one of the bottles they keep on buying, fill it up before they leave the house and refill it throughout the day at work. Doing so would hopefully also reduce trips to the water cooler, and the number of plastic or Styrofoam cups your office consumes in a day.

A little research reveals that there are a number of bottles that can squeeze into skimpy purses and cater to our environmental needs. If size and weight is your main concern, there are clear, collapsible water bottles, that take up no more room than a single folded-up section of newspaper. The smallest size is a 17 oz bottle that weighs about 80 percent less than a regular water bottle. There are also reusable corn-starch containers that look like a normal throwaway water bottle, but actually biodegrade once you discard them. Since they are made from plant matter, they don't leach toxins into the water. They also have a chlorine filter that you can reuse up to 90 times. If you want something that keeps your water cool, the metallic ones are a good bet, and they are extremely durable.

CRT computer monitors

+ **120 lbs**

CO$_2$ per year

In 1946, the ENIAC, one of the world's first computers, weighed 30 metric tons, had 18,000 vacuum tubes, and consumed around 25,000 watts of power. Computers today weigh just a few pounds, and consume between 100 and 150 watts. Monitors consume between 30 and 150 watts depending on the type of screen. Laptops consume even less—about 50 watts—since they can't use too much power or they will overheat.

Computers are one of the most efficient devices in your household. For what they do, they use surprisingly little power. If you haven't already upgraded to LCD (liquid crystal display) monitor, and still use CRT (cathode ray tube) screen, this investment will cut the amount of power it takes to run your computer by about 25 percent.

The advantage of the older CRT technology is they are cheaper, but they are also heavier, bulkier and less adjustable. With LCDs, you can adjust the tilt, height, swivel, or mount them on the wall or on an arm. They use about half as much power as the older screens, and unlike CRT monitors they don't flicker, which reduces eye strain.

Your computer's power usage

- Computer processor (awake): 120 watts
- Computer processor (asleep): 30 watts or less
- CRT Monitor (19 ins screen): 100 watts
- LCD Monitor (19 ins screen): 45 watts
- Laptop: 50 watts

Office lighting

968 lbs

CO$_2$ per year

Lighting is responsible for about one quarter or more of the energy costs in commercial buildings. It usually constitues the single largest part of the electricity bill. Switching to fluorescent lighting is one of the most effective changes you can make to your workplace environment, and will save about 0.9 lbs of CO$_2$ per square foot every year, which for an average-sized office of about 1,076 square feet will add up to a saving of 968 lbs of CO$_2$ a year. If you find the light a little cold, try installing a desk lamp with a green or red spectrum fluorescent bulbs, which are warmer than the blue wavelength often used overhead.

How much natural light do you have in your office? It might sound obvious, but making best use of the available natural light equals energy savings. An office with great natural light in an open plan space uses about 0.7 Watts of power per square foot (W/ft^2)of floor space. Average buildings use around 0.9-1.9 W/ft^2, and poorly planned buildings may use well over 1.9 W/ft^2. Increasing the amount of natural light in your work space also has health benefits as artificial light is harder on your eyes, especially if you are staring at a computer screen all day.

Online newspapers

580 lbs

CO_2 per year

Newspapers are big energy gobblers. To publish a ton of newspapers requires 8,400 gallons of water and about 4,000 kWh of electricity. That's enough electricity to power a 3-bedroom European house for an entire year, or enough energy to heat and cool the average North American home for almost six months. And while it's true that a person doesn't read a ton of newspapers, our daily newspaper reading habits add up. In the UK, national readership is about 14 million people every day. In the United States, around 55 million people read a newspaper daily. That works out to about 99 lbs of newspaper per person per year.

Recycling saves 50 lbs of CO_2 per person per year, but reading on-line goes a step further still. Most major newspapers, including *The New York Times*, *LA Times*, *The Guardian* and *The Telegraph*, have an on-line edition that's free. Many readers have already made the switch. Although newspapers sales have declined, the total readership has never been higher.

Stop wasting paper

- 595 lbs of CO_2 is released from a single person reading a year's worth of newspapers.

- Just 12 lbs of CO_2 is released from the person reading the same amount of news on a personal digital assistant (PDA).

Screen saver

1,090 lbs

CO_2 per year

Screen savers save your screens, but they don't save you any power. A more efficient option is to put the computer and monitor into a sleep mode instead, which will use up to 70 percent less power.

Almost all computers have power saving settings, which save energy without changing the computing power—they work by lowering the computer's frequency or voltage. In the lower power state, the computer dissipates fewer watts, and the battery won't get as hot.

There is also a free software program called CO_2Saver, which adjusts your computer's settings to save as much energy as possible, and tracks how much you and all the people using this program are saving. At the time of publication, the program had saved 434,000 lbs of CO_2, or more than 5,000 trees, and this was increasing by 2,000 lbs per day. The program works by adjusting several settings simultaneously to achieve a more efficient sleep mode, according to Paul Angles, the marketing director of Snap Technologies which publishes CO_2Saver. Unfortunately, it only works with Windows XP and Vista.

Reduce your commute

— **5,940 lbs**

CO_2 per year

Do you enjoy your journey to work? If yes, you're one of the lucky ones. Most of us waste hours every week commuting to and from work, and almost half of us find our commute unsatisfying or stressful, according to a study by the US company CareerBuilder. More than one third of employees would take a pay cut to travel fewer miles.

Some remove the daily headache of the commute by changing jobs, or moving closer to their workplace. But there is another solution. You might be able to move your workplace nearer to your home. It may sound over-ambitious, but that's what is behind a new concept called proximate commuting.

Invented by Gene Mullins, a software developer in Seattle, it is a management program under which large, decentralized employers reassign each voluntary participant to a job location (with the same employer) closer to home in order to reduce commuting distances. Mullins's software, called Proximate Commute Mapper, works by matching the various locations of the employees' homes and company branches and comes up with mutually advantageous moves, which require the consent of both the workers and their managers. Surprisingly, only 20 percent of people employed by multi-branch firms work at the location that's nearest to their residence, according to Mullin's research. For the firefighters he surveyed, only 4 percent worked at the station closest to their home, while some commuted up to 145 miles each way.

Those extra miles are a complete waste, not only of your time but of your money, fuel consumption, and the planet's resources. In the long term, they might also take a toll on your health. Several studies have shown that long-distance commuters suffer from more health problems than those who take short trips to work. Physical symptoms range from headaches and backaches to digestive problems and high blood pressure, according to research published jointly by the Center for Psychotherapy Research in Stuttgart and the University Clinic of Ulm in Germany. Not surprisingly, many of us are eager to cut the time we spend in the car on the way to and from work every day. Proximate commuting could be the way to do it, as each year participating employees could save an average of 6,600 miles, 310 gallons of gas, and 215 hours on their commute.

How to reduce your commute

- Flexible hours. One of the reasons commuting can take so long is that everyone is on the road trying to get to work at the same time. Working flexible hours would mean you could start your day later (or earlier) and avoid the rush-hour traffic.

- Work from home. Try to arrange days where you could work from home and avoid the commute completely.

- Change your job. If your daily commute is becoming a real source of stress you may want to consider changing your job. This isn't always an option if there aren't any job openings in your field close to your home, but it's always worth keeping an eye out.

- Move. This is a slightly more drastic change to your lifestyle, but it could make the commute easier. Make sure you're relatively happy at your current job before you move to be closer to your work. You don't want to change jobs a month later and find yourself miles away from work again.

Single-sided copying

3,300 lbs

CO_2 per year

Switching to double-sided copying is one of those simple adjustments that makes a big difference with very little effort. It even saves money. Why it isn't standard is probably because most machines are set to single-sided as the default setting. The greener option means remembering to change the settings each time you copy, and in the rush of a business day, those sorts of small details can be easily overlooked.

Companies that have had the most success in shrinking their carbon footprint often have an office policy of raising awareness of this and other green issues. Or they have a photocopying machine that has the double-sided setting as the default option. Energy saving photocopiers, such as the Energy Star approved models, which still cost about the same as standard models, have this and other environmentally-friendly features such as automatically switching off after a period of inactivity.

Saving money on a photocopier

Conventional 60 cpm copier on all the time	Energy Star-approved copier
Annual Energy Cost: $315	Annual Energy Cost: $125
Annual Paper Cost: $2,300	Annual Paper Cost: $1,600
Total Cost: $2,615	Total Cost: $1,725
Savings: $0	Savings: $890

Switch off lights

970 lbs

CO_2 per year

You can save an extra 970 lbs of CO_2 just by remembering to turn off the lights when you leave the office. Motion sensor lighting is something you might want to raise with the person in charge; it pays for itself in the long run.

If people find it difficult to remember to turn off the lights, it's worth setting up an office-wide campaign. Try putting up signs around the workplace, or invite an expert or speaker to address this and other environmental issues. Another solution is a switch-off monitor—one person agrees to stay until the rest of the office has gone home, and then walks the halls checking for lights left on, or appliances still plugged in.

In the UK, the 100 Days of Carbon Clean-up is an annual campaign for raising awareness of all the easy actions, such as switching off lights, that have a big impact on climate change. Organized by the Chartered Service of Building Services Engineers, the nation-wide event runs from September to December every year. In 2007, more than 600 businesses signed up. A key part of the initiative is to get businesses to evaluate their carbon footprint and find low-cost measures that will significantly lower their greenhouse gas emissions. One company, Fulcrum Consulting, who blogged about their effort on the British Broadcasting Company's website, managed a 30 percent reduction, or 3.9 metric tons CO_2 in 14 weeks.

Machines on standby

+ **4,738 lbs**

CO_2 per year

Machines left on standby is a bigger contributor to climate change than road transport, at least in Britain, according to the Energy Saving Trust, the UK government-funded body committed to tackling global warming. Up to 90 percent of the total energy use of electronics, such as computers, copiers, faxes, scanners and monitors occurs on standby. Their research found that 75 percent of us habitually waste high levels of energy on a daily basis—leaving appliances plugged on permanent standby and chargeable appliances plugged in once they are fully charged.

In reality, it can be hard to remember to switch everything off, which is why *Time* magazine came up with the brilliant suggestion of a switch-off monitor. It might not sound like the most glamorous work, but worthy causes rarely are. Try having one person walking the office halls every evening to make sure all the all the lights and electronics have been turned off. Obviously, some equipment needs to be left on, but simple training and labeling can tackle that. Too often people see the mass of chords connected to a computer and leave everything on because they aren't sure what should be turned off.

Electronic equipment accounts for 9–15 percent of office energy usage. By reducing the power they consume, you'll not only extend the life of your office equipment, you'll help extend the life of our planet.

Lose the ties

800 lbs —

CO_2 per year

Two years ago, the Japanese government, led by its charismatic leader Prime Minister Junichiro Koizumi, essentially cut 2 million metric tons of CO_2 with the stroke of a pen. The initiative, called "Cool Biz," asked Japanese salarymen to swap their trademark dark blue business suits and ties for open collars and light tropical colors. Government offices were set to 82.4°F compared to a norm of 72.0°F. For office workers who weren't sure what to wear, the government issued a clothing suggestion sheet. And to save the sartorial embarrassment of appearing underdressed, stickers were issued that essentially said "Excuse my attire, I'm doing Cool Biz."

The policy has been a tremendous success. In that first year, Japan shaved an estimated half million metric tons from its rising emissions, and the policy became an annual event. Fashions designers have taken note of the change, introducing new lines of light jackets and shirts with wide collars. There's even a Cool Biz haircut—styled in the shape of a Mohawk.

How temperature affects productivity and saves money

According to a 2004 study by Cornell University professor Alan Hedge, warmer temperatures actually increase productivity, and raising the temperature from 68 to 77°F can:

• Increase overall productivity in the office

• Reduce typing errors by up to 44 percent, and increase overall typing output by 150 percent

• Reduce energy consumption (by turning down the air conditioner), and so also reduce office costs

There are plenty of new products out there for the eco-friendly consumer. In fact, the sheer number of new developments means there are many more great products that haven't been included here. The new ball point pens made from corn starch that biodegrade once you throw them out certainly deserve a mention, as do low-VOC paints and varnishes (volatile organic compounds or VOCs are chemicals that contribute to the chemical formation of ozone which, like carbon dioxide, is a greenhouse gas), but there are many others to look out for as well.

Shopping green doesn't just help the environment. It supports companies who are doing their bit for the environment and prioritizing principles over profits. Sometimes buying green is more expensive, and it can be a tough choice, especially if you have a tight budget. That said, there are also plenty of measures we can easily introduce to our consumer-driven habits that can be done at no cost at all, and some will even save you money, so there really is no excuse for not raising your consumer awareness.

PART FIVE

Greener Consumption

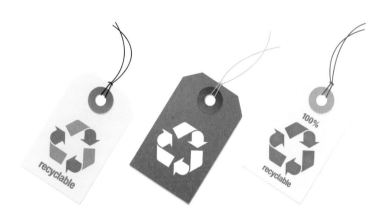

Takeout

40 lbs
CO_2 per year

In our fast-paced consumer culture, it's often hard to find the time to chop some vegetables, get messy, and cook. Which is a shame, because takeout and processed foods often contain more sodium and fats than homemade food and they use more packaging. Several recent studies show that home cooking has benefits beyond the obious ones; for example, it turns out that when children help prepare dinner they are more likely to eat it.

If the thought of quitting (or even cutting down) on takeout fills you with dread, consider the plight of the Colin-Beavan family. The two New Yorkers used to be the epitome of an urban professional life; both worked full-time and ordered in most of their meals. Michelle Colin, a senior writer at the magazine *Business Week*, so rarely cooked that she once called the power company because she couldn't figure out how to turn the oven on. Today, they are the subject of a book and a documentary film. They have given up all take-out meals, carbon-fueled transportation, plastic, paper, television, coffee, and most intriguingly, toilet paper. Food is restricted to organic produce grown within a 25-mile radius of Manhattan. The aim of their elaborate experiment, called "No Impact," is to live carbon and trash free for one year. At the time of publication, they had managed the first nine months, but Mr. Colin had already lost 20 lbs. Wish them luck . . .

Grow your own

40 lbs   —

CO_2 per year

You've probably heard the controversy about food miles; we import far too much of our food, as each piece of food travels an average of 1,346 miles before it reaches your plate, and this is a major contributor to global warming.

Growing your own food is one way to substantially shrink your carbon footprint. It doesn't matter if you don't have a garden—there are special tables available that are ideal for growing a few varieties of herbs and veggies on a balcony or even inside. You don't have to start big; you can begin with just a few potted plants or a small garden and see if you get hooked, as gardeners often do.

One of the great rewards of growing your own vegetables is the sheer number of species you can grow that you could never find in a grocery store. Red Salad Bowl lettuce, Spanish Roja garlic, Ronde de Nice squash; the names are as colorful as the food is flavorful. Glen Clova, Glen Ample, and Glen Moy are three different species of raspberry that are full of taste, easy to gather, and a pleasing shape, size and color. For the best results, talk to other gardeners in your area. Look for species that are well adapted to your local climate. Supermarkets choose fruit and vegetable varieties partly on whether they will pack and keep well in storage, and vegetables that can box well aren't always the ones with the most flavor. In contrast, "heritage" cultivars are grown from seeds that have been passed down from one generation to the next. As a general rule, the taste of these vegetables is stronger and more satisfying than those of their modern successors.

Plastic bags

99 lbs

CO_2 per year

If there is one problem that is an eyesore, a health hazard, and an ecological nightmare around the world, it is the scourge of plastic bags. First introduced in the 1970s, plastic bags became ubiquitous mostly because they are convenient, versatile, and cheap. They cost about a quarter of what it costs to produce a paper bag, they are more durable, use fewer resources to manufacture than paper equivalents, and they are lighter, so they lower the fuel costs of transportation.

With their growth in popularity, disposal became a problem. Every year, between 500 billion and 1 trillion plastic bags are distributed worldwide and less than 3 percent of those bags are recycled. Most plastic bags end up in landfills, where they can take up to 1,000 years to biodegrade, emitting toxins into the soil as they decompose. Those that don't make it to the dump find their way to the world's oceans where they suffocate the aquatic life, or out into parks, bush, or scrubland. Once out in nature, they deface the natural environment, or they are eaten by grazing animals, and can clog up the animal's digestive tract which is potentially lethal. Even once they have passed through an animal, they can still cause environmental damage, as they continue to leach pollutants into the soil, or the scraps of plastic get eaten again. In cities, they clog drains, flap in trees, and litter neighborhoods. In Africa, they are also a health hazard, as they spread malaria by holding mini-pools of warm water for mosquitoes to breed in.

Faced with these environmental concerns, Ireland, Taiwan, South Africa, Australia, San Francisco, and Bangladesh have heavily taxed the totes or banned their use outright. In Rwanda and Eritrea, the bags are severely restricted—if you carry a plastic bag into the airport in Kigali, it will be confiscated.

Whatever the law, it's not hard to make a big dent in the plastic bag problem. Next time you go shopping, try taking a cloth bag with you instead of having the cashier give you plastic. If you find it hard to remember, write a note to yourself on the fridge or the front door until it becomes a habit. Reuse the old plastic bags you have lying around—they make good garbage liners or use the smaller ones for filling up with fresh produce at the veggie section of the grocery store. And remember, when you feel like buying anything, BYOB.

International plastic taxes and bans

- In Ireland, a tax on plastic bags, introduced in 2002, has cut their use by more than 95 percent. The "plas tax" has also raised millions of euros, to be used for environmental projects.

- In Taiwan, there are large fines against businesses that give away plastic bags, utensils, and Styrofoam and plastic food containers. Since the laws were introduced in 2003, plastic bag use has fallen by 69 percent drop, and the use of plastic cutlery by 90 percent.

- Denmark introduced a packaging tax in 1994. Consumption of paper and plastic bags has declined by 66 percent.

- Bangladesh slapped an outright ban on all polythene bags in 2002 after they were found to have been the main culprit during the 1988 and 1998 floods that submerged two-thirds of the country. Discarded bags had choked the country's drainage systems.

Paper towel

 # 150 lbs

CO_2 per year

Imagine for a brief second that you're in a public restroom. You've washed your hands and now before you are two choices, the paper towel or the dryer. You hesitate—which is the greener option? The calculation is complicated as there are many factors to take into account, such as transport and disposal costs, but in a recent study, paper towels were found to use nearly three times more global warming gases than the dryer. According to a 2001 report by Environmental Resource Management, the towels also create about seven times more smog pollutants.

Paper towels require fossil fuels and bleach to manufacture and the production emits greenhouse gases. Environmentally, you are better off using a sponge to wipe up spills since it can be reused many times. If you do decide to buy paper towel, go for the recycled option since it uses less water and energy to produce and causes fewer carbon emissions. Look for brands with a high percentage of recycled content (90 percent or more) since some claim to be environmentally friendly, but have less than 5 percent recycled content.

How using recycled paper towel reduces waste

If every household in the US replaced just one roll of 180-sheet virgin-fiber paper towels with 100-percent recycled paper towels, it would save:

• 1.4 million trees

• 3.7 million cubic feet of landfill space

• 526 million gallons of water

• 89,400 pounds of pollution

Recycle paper

110 lbs —

CO_2 per year

There are many good reasons to buy recycled paper and recycle the paper you buy. We throw away more paper than anything else every day. For every 100 lbs of trash we discard, 35 lbs of it is paper. Newspapers alone account for 14 percent of landfill space, according to the US Government's Energy Information Administration. The paper used for packaging accounts for another 15 to 20 percent.

Recycled paper saves resources. Compared to virgin pulp, it uses 35 percent less water and produces 74 percent less air pollution. It also consumes between 10 and 30 percent less energy. That means for 1 lb of paper that you recycle, you save 0.9 lbs of CO_2 emissions. And for each ream of paper you replace with recycled, you save 5 lbs of carbon dioxide.

One of the pollutants used to bleach paper is chlorine, which is a known carcinogen, and poisonous to aquatic environments. Chlorine is used in both the treatment of virgin and recycled paper, but there are less toxic substitutes. To ensure you buy paper that hasn't been processed with chlorine, look out for sheets and pads marked with TCF (totally chlorine-free) or PCF (processed chlorine-free).

Local food

5,000 lbs
CO_2 per year

There are some eating experiences you never forget. Sometimes it is those that are extremely painful: a Jalapeno bitten whole before realizing that it wasn't a bell pepper, or a spoonful of Wasabi mistaken for guacamole. And then there are those food memories that stand out because the first bite sends a shiver of sensuous pleasure along your tongue and tastebuds, a regular experience for consumers of local food.

For those uninitiated to buying produce locally, now is the time to make your way down to the nearest farmer's market and try the squash or tomatoes—whatever is in season. Then compare it to the lesser equivalents that have traveled thousands of miles from overseas to reach your grocery store. The difference in taste should be fairly obvious: a snow pea grown by a local farmer and never refrigerated will retain more of its delicate flavor than one shipped in a plane from Guatemala. You don't have to take my word for it—just ask any number of the world's top chefs who buy local food in order to have the best possible ingredients. By eating locally you're not just getting food of a higher quality, you're also supporting your local farmers and producers. While at the same time the fuel costs and emissions of transportation are virtually cut out, which can add up to a total carbon saving of 5,000 lbs a year, just by having local food once a week.

If you live in a northern climate, eating locally is much harder in the winter than summer. There are also some foods, like tea and coffee, that probably don't grow anywhere near you live. Some environmentalists cut out these foods anyway—the 100-mile and 250-mile diets specify the acceptable distance produce can travel for it to be deemed edible (the distances are based on the number of miles a farmer can travel on horseback in one day). But these diets are only for really hardcore converts; most foodies who eat locally believe there should be some give and take about the whole project. The purpose is to help the planet, not to make life unbearably difficult.

In choosing what to eat, even small steps make a difference. Try eating locally grown food just once a week. By becoming part of the local-food market, you help the farmers who are trying to bring the freshest ingredients to our tables, most of whom go out of their way to make sure their food is produced in a sustainable way. And while doing your part for the planet, you get to please the palate too.

Statistics for imported food

- On average, fresh produce travels around 1,500 miles from its source to your plate.

- A typical meal in the US contains ingredients from at least five countries outside the US.

- In the UK, half of the vegetables and 95 percent of the fruit are imported.

- In the US, 12 percent of the vegetables and 39 percent of the fruits are imported.

- 30 percent of the vehicles on our roads are currently transporting food.

Plastic cutlery

4 lbs
CO_2 per year

If you use plastic cutlery once a week you are adding 4 lbs of carbon dioxide a year to our environment. That may not be a lot compared to long-distance flying, say, but plastic cutlery is very easy to live without, and what's more has been linked to health concerns in dozens of studies. It is usually made from either polycarbonate plastic, polystyrenes, or styrenes. The building block of polycarbonate plastic is bisphenol A, which is used in the production of many consumer products including most baby bottles. In mice and rats, there is evidence that even very low doses of bisphenol A can cause disrupted reproductive cycles, abnormal sexual behavior, hyperactivity, increased fat formation, early puberty, and structural damage to the brain. The danger is that hot or fatty substances can dissolve traces of this chemical into the food.

Polystyrene and styrenes are used to make a variety of containers, including foam cups, yogurt and deli containers, and clear plastic cookie trays. Chemicals called dioxins are generated during this material's manufacture and can leach into foods and liquids when in contact with this plastic. Dioxins have been linked to cancer, immune dysfunction, IQ deficit, and reproductive defects. They were considered the most dangerous ingredient of Agent Orange, the chemical defoliant that was used in Vietnam; several studies have linked these toxins to the increased rates of birth deformities in those that were exposed to the herbicide.

Corn plastic

1.5 lbs ▬

CO_2 per lb of plastic

The first forays into corn-based plastics began in the 1930s, but until recently the industry has found it difficult to make a material that could compete on cost. An earlier effort in the mid-80s of supposedly "biodegradable" plastic broke down into small fragments of polyethylene, which was a disaster for the people's home compost bins.

However, a new material made from corn has started hitting supermarket shelves, replacing plastic containers. Polyactic acid (abbreviated to PLA or just corn plastic) is cheaper, biodegrades in your compost in 90 days, and doesn't leach the toxins associated with PET plastic. It also takes 68 percent fewer greenhouse gases to produce. It is increasingly used to make water bottles, sandwich containers, labels, electronics casings, wrap for flowers, clothing fiber, and pillow stuffing.

Currently, only certain stores stock the new material and only for certain products, but while this plastic is not available everywhere, it is rapidly making inroads as retailers respond to environmentally aware consumers. Buying corn plastic products will help speed that process along.

Bottled water

110 lbs

CO_2 per year

Bottled water was once the ultimate luxury accessory. Flown in from Italy, Fuji, or France, distilled from a mountain glacier or ancient springs, it has become a global business that has seen great expansion in the past decade. Some of the finest restaurants in the world even provide water sommeliers so their clientele can find out which water to drink with their gourmet meal.

Whatever the brand, bottled water takes a tremendous toll on the environment. It takes oil to make the plastic in all those bottles, oil to run the bottling factory, and more oil to transport the water to the consumer, and each of these stages generates more greenhouse gases. The US-based Natural Resources Defense Council estimates that 8 million lbs of CO_2 is generated each year just by importing bottled water. Producing the plastic bottles also uses up the planet's water. According to Rick Smith, the executive director of Toronto-based Environmental Defence, the production of 1 lb of PET plastic requires 18 lbs of water and results in emissions of over half a dozen significant pollutants, including carbon dioxide, nitrogen oxides, carbon monoxide, and sulphur oxides.

The migration toward an increased use of bottled water often fosters a perception that tap water is less safe than its bottled equivalent, but some studies now suggest that the opposite is true. In a recent report, William Shotyk, a scientist working at the University of Heidelberg, released an analysis of 132 brands of bottled water. The chemist examined the contaminants in PET, the most common type of plastic used to make the bottles. After the bottles had been stored for six months, Shotyk found that significant levels of antimony, a toxic chemical used in the bottle's production, had leached into the water. Shotyk is now studying the bottles over a longer period of time, given the lag times that can occur between the bottling process, shipping, purchase, and consumption. He has also vowed that he will never drink bottled water again. That's a choice we should all consider, Smith says. "Bottled water is a not only a complete disaster for the environment but potentially for human health. There is increasing evidence that the plastic actually leaches toxic ingredients into the water itself."

So when you're out and about, try and remember to fill up a reusable bottle with tap water to take out with you so you don't have to waste anymore of your money or our planet's resources on bottled water.

Why avoid bottled water?

- It is far more expensive than tap water, costing anywhere from 240 to 10,000 times more. In fact a gallon of bottled water would work out more expensive than a gallon of gas for your car.

- In most cases bottled water is not purer or better for you than drinkable tap water. Almost 40 percent of bottled water should be labeled bottled tap water because that is exactly what it is.

- Most bottled water is imported and is often transported thousands of miles to reach its destination.

- Around 80 percent of bottles are not recycled. They are thrown away and end up in landfill sites where they can take hundreds of years to biodegrade.

Vintage fashion

800 lbs

CO_2 per year

Buying second hand clothes lowers your carbon footprint by eliminating the energy taken to produce something new. Every item of clothing you own has an impact on the environment. For example, some synthetic fabrics are made with petroleum products. Natural products don't use fossil fuels to produce, but there can be other concerns. For example, the world's cotton is responsible for 3 percent of farmed land, but cotton production consumes 16 percent of the world's pesticides, more than any other single crop. Unless you live in China, which dominates the clothing import market, energy is required to ship the item from wherever it was produced—it all adds up.

Don't assume that just because it's second hand it means it is second rate—you can get some great deals on vintage and designer clothes, so get searching! And don't forget to recycle your own clothes instead of throwing them out. Even if your old shirts aren't designer fashion, there are still plenty of charities that will welcome the donation.

Energy consumption of new clothes

- Producing a pair of men's polyester pants requires about 50 kWh of energy and releases 67 lbs of CO_2.

- One lb of cotton clothing takes 30 kWh to produce and emits 40 lbs of CO_2.

- The average person goes through 24 lbs of cotton per year.

- It takes 39 times as much energy to produce a cotton shirt from scratch as it does to recycle a similar shirt.

Disposable diapers

59 lbs

CO$_2$ per year

In terms of sheer convenience, disposable diapers are hard to beat. You use them once and toss them—then the trash collector takes them away. But before succumbing to the easiest option, there are a few sobering facts.

In the US alone, 3.5 billion gallons of oil are used to produce the nation's annual consumption of diapers. The average child uses over 5,000 diapers before they are toilet trained. Those diapers create waste that accounts for about 3 percent of all landfill space.

When people think about cloth diapers, they probably imagine soiled cotton wraps boiling away on the kitchen stove. Thankfully, cloth diapers have come a long way in the past thirty years, and today they look more like a pair of colorful briefs than a swaddling band held together with safety pins. They are water-proof and machine-washable, and if you can't face washing them yourself, there are diaper laundering services, although it's debatable whether this option actually saves any energy—some studies say it still does, others say the emissions of a laundering services outweigh the savings of using cloth diapers.

If you don't mind machine washing your baby's diapers, cloth diapers are environmentally the best option, according to several studies including a report by the Landbank Consultancy, an independent London environmental agency. They found that disposable diapers use 20 times more raw materials, three times more energy, twice as much water, and generate 60 times more waste. If cloth diapers still aren't for you, biodegradable diapers are also better than the disposables, and most stores stock them, or you can easily find them online.

Cheeseburgers

6 lbs

CO_2 per year per cheeseburger

If you love a burger, you're in good company. On average, North Americans eat about three hamburgers each week or about 150 burgers per year. An individual hamburger doesn't use up much CO_2 if you eat it at home— a mere 0.4 lbs—but at your local fast food joint, the carbon cost is much greater.

Measuring the carbon cost of what goes into a cheeseburger—from the energy used to manufacture the milk to make the cheese, to the cost of canning cucumbers for pickles—is probably more detail than you bargained for, but a joint report by Stockholm University and the Swiss Institute of Technology investigated these issues. Published in 2000, the researchers conclude that the total energy going into a single cheeseburger is between about 7 and 20 megajoules; the range results from the different methods used in the food industry. Once you include the greenhouse gases produced in running the restaurant, and the carbon consumed in driving there, it costs between 6.3 to 6.8 lbs of carbon emissions to eat a single cheeseburger from your local fast food restaurant. That's without the side of fries.

Organic food

1,000 lbs

CO_2 per year

If just one quarter of your fresh produce is organic you could save 1,000 lbs of carbon dioxide per year. With the rise of the green movement, organic food sales have skyrocketed. In the United States, they have grown by 17–20 percent per year, compared to 2–3 percent for conventional foods. In the UK organic food has done even better, growing by more than 20 percent each year, and 30 percent in the year 2006.

One of the benefits of this growth is that many products have come down in price. Compared to five years ago, it's now much easier to buy organic without breaking the bank. Unfortunately, cheapest doesn't necessarily mean best. The organic food that's shipped in from abroad can cost less than the same product grown locally, although the carbon cost of transportation means it's much worse for the environment.

Organic fruits and veggies are free from pesticides, artificial fertilizers, food additives, human waste, or sewage sludge. Organic livestock must be reared without the routine use of antibiotics or growth hormones. In most countries, organic produce can't be genetically modified. Since some of the chemicals used in pesticides and growth hormones have been linked to cancer, at least in mice and rats, some scientists believe organic food is better for your health. There are also studies that suggest organic foods contain higher levels of vitamins than their conventionally grown counterparts, since good quality soil produces healthier plants. However, these relationships are complex and require further study before we know for sure. In contrast, the link between locally grown organics and less greenhouse gases is already crystal clear.

Less meat

—
3,924 lbs

CO_2 per year

Which contributes more to climate change: driving an SUV or serving steaks for supper? Believe it or not, it's the beef. The international meat industry generates roughly 18 percent of the world's greenhouse-gas emissions. That's more than the total for the transportation, which is responsible for 13 percent according to a report released last year by the UN's Food and Agriculture Organization (FAO).

Industrial farming is a complex, multistage, energy-hungry industry. It takes fossil fuels to manufacture the fertilizer, run the farm machinery, ferry the animals to the abattoir, and all the other steps that go into producing the packaged and sealed cuts we buy from our grocery store. Taken together, these practices release 9 percent of human-produced carbon dioxide.

Methane gas is also a global-warming accelerator: it traps 21 times more heat than cardon dioxide. Breeding and caring for farm animals accounts for 37 percent of human-produced methane and 64 percent of human-produced nitrous oxide. Nitrous oxide is even worse than methane for climate change as it stores 296 times more heat than carbon dioxide. These gases not only contribute to global warming, they cause other problems for our environment as well. Even though it is measured in the atmosphere in parts per billion, nitrous oxide can overwhelm forests, producing what the FAO calls "forest dieback." The excessive nitrogen load essentially reverses the growth effect of carbon dioxide and reduces the capacity of forests to act as "carbon sinks."

Rearing livestock also takes up much of the earth's prime real-estate. Livestock commands 30 percent of the planet's land surface, and 70 percent of the planet's entire agricultural land. These numbers are disportionately high and it takes more land to feed a population on a meat-based diet than a vegetarian one.

These figures are expected to rise rapidly over the next decade if current trends continue. Economic growth in developing countries has driven the world's recent rise in meat production, and the higher the income, the bigger the steaks tend to be. On average Canadians and Americans consume around 220 lbs of meat per person every year, which requires the killing of 10 billion animals. China accounts for 60 percent of the world's increase in meat production in the past 25 years and is now the world's biggest producer of pork and, correspondingly, the world's biggest producer of methane gas from pig manure.

These facts don't bode well for the New York strip steaks or summer barbeques. But if we all cut our meat consumption by a third, we're more likely to inherit a cleaner and greener earth.

How your diet affects emissions

- The average meat diet results in an extra 1.5 metric tons of greenhouse gases a year compared to a vegetarian diet.

- Annual global meat production is projected to double from 229 million metric tons at the start of the decade to 465 million metric tons by 2050.

- The major pollutants from raising livestock are animal wastes like methane, antibiotics and hormones, chemicals from tanneries, fertilizers and the pesticides used to spray feed crops.

- These pollutants affect the world's air and water resources, contributing to reservoir and lake contamination, euthropication and the degeneration of coral reefs.

Organic cotton

— **25 lbs**

CO_2 per year

Cotton has been one of the world's favorite materials for centuries. It's cheap, strong, and lightweight—ideal for products as diverse as bed sheets and cotton swabs. But while its shirts clothe our backs, its production takes a tremendous toll on the health of this planet. The world's cotton industry is responsible for 3 percent of global cropland, but 16 percent of its insecticide use, more than any other single crop. Many of the chemicals sprayed on cotton, such as the two common insecticides deltamethrin and endosulfan, are considered hazardous by the World Health Organization. Others, like Aldicarb—common in cotton production in the US—is considered extremely hazardous and is banned in some parts of the world. At high doses these pesticides can cause nausea, tremors, excessive sweating, dizziness, skin rashes, headaches, or blurred vision.

In the last decade, there has been a growing awareness of the problems of cotton farming. The alternative, organic cotton, has become a more viable option. Currently, it accounts for just a fraction (0.15 percent) of the total production, but it has seen a rapid expansion in the past few years. You can now find stores that are stocking some products such as organic shirts, T-shirts and some baby wear, and others have started to use a blend of organic and regular cotton in some of their clothing lines. You too could make your first foray into using this sustainable material by buying organic bed sheets. If you switch one quarter of your clothes for organic cotton ones, you'll save about 25 lbs of CO_2.

Pre-packaged lunches

150 lbs

CO$_2$ per year

Like most foods, the lunch box has as much to do with taste and nutrition as it does convenience and compromise. Some parents choose to go completely waste-free and eliminate all packaging, but this isn't an easy choice; It can be hard to find a yogurt container that doesn't leak or a kid who wants to eat a wrapper-less chocolate bar.

However, even for those of us who are time-pressured and cost-aware, there are a number of small steps that will really cut down on garbage. On average, a year's worth of lunches creates 67 lbs of paper and plastic waste. Much of this is easily avoidable, by cutting out products like ziplock bags or paper napkins.

Dos	Don'ts
• Store food like sandwiches and fruit in reusable and washable containers or reuse Ziplock bags	• Buy prepackaged cheeses, fruit snacks, or puddings
• Buy foods like cookies or chips in bulk not in individual portions	• Buy disposable juice boxes, juice pouches, soda cans, water bottles, and milk cartons
• Use cloth, not paper napkins	• Pack plastic forks and spoons. (see entry 88 for concerns on disposal and health with certain)
• Pack a drink in a water-tight, fully sealed, washable bottle	• Use paper napkins, or brown paper bags
• Use a washable, reusable lunchbox	• Use vinyl lunch boxes, since they may contain lead
• Wrap food in wax paper as it biodegrades quickly	

Green wedding

8,818 lbs

CO_2 on the day

Stories about green weddings usually focus on a couple who choose a vegan menu and go hiking for the pre-wedding date. Unless you are a very committed environmentalist, these sorts of suggestions are probably a bit intimidating. Not everyone who cares about the planet wants to eat bean curd on one of the most important days of his or her life; nor should they have to. A wedding is a time to celebrate with friends and family and your happiness should come first. That said, the average wedding creates 16 metric tons of carbon dioxide emissions, and there are many things one can do that make a big difference without sacrificing your big day.

How to have a green wedding

- Try and have your wedding at a local venue to reduce the distance your guests have to drive (or fly).

- For the invitations, you could choose paper made from recycled cotton or wool that doesn't use as many chemicals in the production process.

- Do a bit of research on your ring; you don't want to mistakenly invest in a blood diamond or gold that polluted the natural environment through open pit mining.

- Register for greener gifts such as Energy Star rated products or organic bed linen.

- Weddings are often unnecessarily large affairs. On average 178 guests will attend a wedding and if you could cut that number by a third, you could save 8,818 lbs of CO_2.

Library books

30 lbs

CO_2 per year

—

Book manufacture, like almost all industries, takes energy, electricity, and fossil fuel burning power that emits carbon dioxide and other greenhouse gases. Each book takes many processes to bring it to publication—the receipt and editing of manuscripts, which involves computers and printers, heating and air conditioning, lighting, pens and paper, and telephones. Turning those manuscripts into the pages of a book involves chopping down trees, debarking the wood, and pulping it for the printers. Each of these stages requires energy and emissions to transport the materials, whether ferrying the wood, the pulp, paper, or the books themselves to storage warehouses and book stores. Taken together, all these stages add up, totaling about 5.5 lbs of CO_2 per paperback, according to Penguin Books.

Of course, we're not going to stop reading books, but you don't have to buy them all. So for book junkies, there are a number of ways to feed an addiction while reducing your carbon footprint. Libraries are a good place to start, or sharing books among friends. Second hand stores are usually a great idea for reducing your carbon footprint and are usually cheaper than buying brand new. You can browse used bookstores from the comfort of your own home via the internet, for example Abebooks is similar to eBay and it brings together 13,500 used book sellers from around the world.

Extra packaging

2,400 lbs

CO_2 per year

Between 1970 and 2005, the average amount of garbage per person rose by 102 percent. In the past 15 years, despite growing environmental awareness, it has risen by 20 percent. Today, each person creates 1,620 lbs of waste per year in the United States and 1,301 lbs in Europe.

Wherever you live, you can cut down on the amount of waste you throw away every year by avoiding products with packaging. In the grocery store, don't use plastic bags for smaller items such as cucumbers, bulbs of garlic, or lemons; bring your own plastic bags to the shop instead (see entry 83). Try to avoid packaging made with mixed materials, such as paper laminated with plastic or foil, since they are hard to recycle. Cut down on processed food—it contains more sodium and uses yet more packaging. When shipping something, bring old Styrofoam packing peanuts and bubble wrap to the post office.

Packaging waste: the United States vs. the European Union

Category	United States	European Union
Population	290,810,000	382,300,000
Municipal waste per capita in lbs	1,620	1,301
Packaging waste per capita in lbs	520	388
Packaging waste per capita percentage of total produced	32	30

Carbon offsets

800 lbs —

CO_2 per year

Carbon offsetting is the idea of paying for carbon emissions elsewhere instead of reducing them. If for example you were unable to avoid taking a long-distance flight, you could purchase carbon offsets to compensate for the carbon emissions of the flight. The money you spend is put toward environmental projects such as tree planting projects or renewable energy inniatives. Most environmentalists argue that the best way to lower your emissions is not to produce them at all and that you can't buy your way out of your responsibility. However, we're all human, and we all have to live, work, and have fun, so at some point we might decide to purchase offsets to compensate for the climate change gases we have produced.

Finding an organization that sells offsets is very easy. Not surprisingly, there are many organizations that will happily take your money, especially when the final product is as nebulous as greenhouse gases that weren't produced. The price of offsets also varies greatly, which has caused problems for buyers, as sometimes they are charged far more for credit carbons than other companies are offering for the exact same quantity.

One of the difficulties is that the carbon credit market is very new, and the standards are still evolving. To help customers make good choices, an international standard, called the Gold Standard, was set up to rate different offset options. It ensures that key environmental criteria have been met by offset projects that carry its label, and only includes offsets from energy efficiency and renewable energy projects, so projects such as tree planting do not qualify. It also includes social indicators to make sure your money goes towards sustainable development.

Conclusion

It is particularly difficult to write a conclusion for this book. The world is currently at a critical juncture and the choices we make will shape what our future holds. The ending hasn't been written yet, since we have only just started to live with the beginnings of global warming. The earth's average global surface temperature is 1.2°F warmer than it was before the Industrial Revolution. Carbon dioxide levels in the atmosphere have also increased to 377 parts per million (ppm), compared to 280 ppm before the nineteenth century. How much more carbon dioxide we can pump into the atmosphere before the earth can no longer return to its state of equilibrium is an important question that some of the world's leading scientists are addressing. "Avoiding Dangerous Climate Change," a 2006 report by the UK government, suggested that levels should be stabilized at about 450 ppm or below before the change becomes irreversible. The European Union has recommended 550 ppm as a suitable goal.

To ensure that carbon dioxide levels and temperatures do not reach the crucial tipping point, businesses, legislators, scientists, and private individuals must all make climate change a priority. As a private citizen, you have a number of options. You can reduce your carbon footprint with just a few simple changes to your lifestyle. You can help shape what products the stores stock on their shelves by buying those that are eco-friendly. Part Five lists some of these alternatives, but it's also worth doing a bit of your own research as there are many more eco-friendly products available now than this book could cover. You can also lobby legislators or join charities that have made these issues a priority, because on certain issues, such as the emission laws for heavy industry or the quality of public transit, real change must come through legislative action.

Climate change sometimes seems like a slow-moving tsunami. We can see it steadily approaching from the distance, gathering speed and vigor as we continue with our daily lives. Yet we continue to leave the lights and heating on in every room, to drive our kids to school, to tear through product packaging without a second thought, and to jet about the world on business trips and holidays. We've been told that it will hit at some point and that the impacts will change the world as we know it, but since no one else seems to worry, why should we? For some reason, the idea that in twenty years we might not be able to live the same energy-extravagant lifestyle doesn't seem to move us—and yet it must, for this is the issue that will define the twenty-first century, and shape our future and that of the planet. The only possible time to act is now.

Resources

PART ONE

1. New carpets

http://www.isdesignet.com/articles/detail.aspx?contentID=4749
http://www.metrokc.gov/procure/green/carpet.htm

2. Microwave

http://www.aceee.org/consumerguide/cooking.htm
http://www.eere.energy.gov/buildings/appliance_standards/resid
ential/pdfs/kitchen_products.pdf
http://www.time.com/time/specials/2007/environment/article/0,2
8804,1602354_1603074_1603636,00.html

3. Energy audit

http://unstats.un.org/unsd/cdb/cdb_series_xrxx.asp?series_cod
e=30248
http://www.eia.doe.gov/oiaf/1605/ggrpt/carbon.html
http://www.guardian.co.uk/environment/2007/jun/19/china.usne
ws
http://www.thehcf.org/emaila5.html
http://www.ucsusa.org/publications/greentips/whats-your-
carb.html

4. Air leaks

http://www.energycodes.gov/training/consumer_ed/air_leaks.stm
http://www.energystar.gov/index.cfm?c=products.es_at_home_
tips
http://www.greenergyglobal.com/pages/articles/feature3.php

5. Go tankless

http://www.aceee.org/consumerguide/
http://www.eere.energy.gov/consumer/your_home/water_heatin
g/index.cfm/mytopic=13020

6. Double meals

http://health.msn.com/dietfitness/ArticlePage.aspx?cp-
documentid=100171934
http://www.carbonrationing.org.uk/maryland/threads/overview-
reduce-carbon-save-money-join-the-maryland-crag
http://ohioline.osu.edu/hyg-fact/5000/pdf/5402.pdf
http://www.nutrition.com.sg/atd/atdcooking.asp

7. Leaky faucets

http://www.energystar.gov/index.cfm?c=products.es_at_home_
tips
Godo S. *The Carbon Buster's Home Energy Handbook*, Gabriola
Island, British Columbia: New Society Publishers, 2007.

8. Energy Star

http://www.energystar.gov/
http://www.iwrc.org/downloads/pdf/CoalPowerPlantsEmissions
Facts.pdf

9. Full dishwasher

http://ces.ca.uky.edu/lincoln/fcs/How%20to%20Conserve%20E
nergy%20with%20Appliances.pdf

10. Clogged AC filter

http://www.energystar.gov/ia/partners/prod_development/revisio
ns/downloads/ac_ashp/American%20Council%20for%20an%2
0Energy-Efficient%20Economy%20(ACEEE)2.pdf
http://www.energystar.gov/index.cfm?c=heat_cool.pr_hvac
http://www.oee.nrcan.gc.ca/publications/infosource/pub/energy
_use/air-conditioning-
home2004/roomac.cfm?text=N&printview=N

11. Go fluorescent

http://www.aceee.org/consumerguide/lighting.htm
Ewoldt J. Dollars & Sense: Fluorescent evolution. *Star-Tribune*,
August 14 2007
Prescott M. Bright lights: Still not convinced by the
performance of eco light blubs? Matt Prescott founder of the
Ban the Bulb campaign, puts the latest models to the test. *The
Guardian*, August 2, 2007
Roges L. Architects role in shedding light on solar power
design. *Real Estate Weekly*, August 8, 2007

12. Two fridges

http://www.aceee.org/consumerguide/refrigeration.htm
http://ces.ca.uky.edu/lincoln/fcs/How%20to%20Conserve%20E
nergy%20with%20Appliances.pdf
http://observer.guardian.co.uk/magazine/story/0,,1992556,00.ht
ml

13. Hug your water heater

http://www.aceee.org/consumerguide/
http://www.energystar.gov/

14. Eco-flooring

Cupolo D. Floored by the choices cork, bamboo and other
green floors. *The Star-Ledger*, August 30, 2007
Hom K. Greening the gear; bamboo bikes and sustainable
skateboards put a new spin on sports. *The Washington Post*,
September 11 2007
http://news.bbc.co.uk/2/hi/asia-pacific/6277518.stm

http://www.panda.org/about_wwf/where_we_work/europe/what_we_do/mediterranean/about/forests/cork/index.cfm

15. Green power
http://www.ecotricity.co.uk/
http://www.eere.energy.gov/greenpower/

16. Larger homes
http://www.time.com/time/specials/2007/environment/article/0,28804,1602354_1603074_1603123,00.html
White R. Housing needs space-saving creativity; How much do we really need? *The Calgary Herald*, July 28, 2007

17. Ice build-up
http://www.aceee.org/consumerguide/refrigeration.htm

18. Insulate walls and roofs
http://www.eere.energy.gov/consumer/your_home/insulation_air sealing/index.cfm/mytopic=11220
http://www.energystar.gov/index.cfm?c=home_sealing.hm_improvement_sealing

19. Cold wash
http://www.aceee.org/consumerguide/laundry.htm
http://www.energystar.gov/index.cfm?c=clotheswash.pr_clothes_washers

20. Air-conditioning
http://www.cenerg.ensmp.fr/english/themes/syst/html/cles.htm
http://www.thegreenguide.com/blog/lighten-up

21. Clothes dryer
Hotton P. Venting gas dryers; keeping pipes from freezing. *The Boston Globe*, 22 February 2007
http://www.pembina.org
Steffen, A. *Worldchanging: A User's Guide for the 21st Century*, New York, NY; Harry N. Abrams, Inc, 2006
Tsong N. A hip, modern clothesline can turn your laundry green. *Seattle Times*, 4 August 2007

22. Sustainable wood
www.fscus.org/
Hom K. Greening the gear; bamboo bikes and sustainable skateboards put a new spin on sports.

23. Cook with gas
http://www.aceee.org/consumerguide/cooking.htm

www.canwesavetheworld.com/reduce-residential-energy-use.html
Goodall C. *How to Lead a Low Carbon Life*, London, England: Earthscan Publications Ltd, 2007

24. Unplug it
http://ces.ca.uky.edu/lincoln/fcs/How%20to%20Conserve%20Energy%20with%20Appliances.pdf
http://www.energysavingtrust.org.uk/aboutest/news/pressreleases/index.cfm?mode=view&press_id=451
http://news.bbc.co.uk/2/hi/science/nature/4620350.stm

25. Long showers
http://www.pioneerwest.net/sf06outcomereport.pdf
http://www.thegreenguide.com

26. Recycling
http://cahe.nmsu.edu/pubs/_g/G-314.pdf
http://www.mbdc.com/challenge/Cradle-To-Cradle_Design_Guidelines.pdf

27. Wear a sweater
http://www.aceee.org/consumerguide/heating.htm

28. Hot water
http://www.aboutkidshealth.ca/HealthAZ/Burn-Safety-Hot-Water-Temperature.aspx?articleID=8652&categoryID=
http://www.aceee.org/consumerguide/waterheating.htm

29.LED tree lights.
http://www.colorkinetics.com/
http://www.timesonline.co.uk/tol/life_and_style/health/complementary_medicine/article754483.ece

PART TWO
30. City living
Holtzclaw J. Making truth convenient: Ending Our Oil Addiction, Building Sustainable Communities. National Student Conference, Washington, D.C., July 12, 2006

31. Patio porch heater
McCarthy M. Enemy of the planet. *The Independent*, July 26, 2007
http://www.population.health.wa.gov.au/environmental/resources/Patio%20Heaters.pdf

32. Compost
http://www.cat.org.uk/information/catinfo.tmpl?command=searc

h&db=catinfo.db&eqSKUdatarq=InfoSheet_CompostingForClim
ate
http://www.carbonzero.ca
http://women.timesonline.co.uk/tol/life_and_style/women/body_
and_soul/article1679066.ece

33. Double glazing
http://www.eere.energy.gov/consumer/your_home/windows_do
ors_skylights/index.cfm/mytopic=13330
http://www.glassforeurope.com/issues/building/EnergyAndEnvir
onment/Pages/lowedoubleglazing.aspx
Goodall, *How to Lead a Low Carbon Life*

34. Rain harvesting
http://www.achievegreen.com/category/energy/
http://www.savetherain.info/media-centre/rainwater-harvesting-
faqs.aspx
Stoyke, *The Carbon Buster's Home Energy Handbook*
http://women.timesonline.co.uk/tol/life_and_style/women/body_
and_soul/article1679066.ece
http://www.wrexham.gov.uk/english/env_services/community_s
ervices/waterbutts.cfm

35. Leaf blowers
Lifsher M. Firms Fight Over Rules On Tools. *The Wall Street
Journal*, March 11, 1998
http://cobweb.businesscollaborator.com/cclevy/mb/mbinfo_12.h
tm
http://www.time.com/time/specials/2007/environment/article/0,2
8804,1602354_1603074_1603631,00.html

37. Plant a tree
http://www.arborday.org/globalwarming/
http://esa21.kennesaw.edu/activities/trees-carbon/trees-
carbon.pdf
http://forestmanagement.enr.gov.nt.ca/forest_education/amazin
g_tree_facts.htm
http://query.nytimes.com/gst/fullpage.html?res=990DE3D8103C
F933A05752C0A9669C8B63&sec=&spon=&pagewanted=all

38. Day watering
http://www.redcross.org/static/file_cont162_lang0_70.pdf
http://www.state.nj.us/drbc/drought/kids_whatyoucando.htm

39. Wind turbine
http://windustry.org/

40. Community garden
http://www.gardenmosaics.cornell.edu/
Mirosch N. Green footprint. *The Courier-Mail*, September 11,
2007
http://www.foodshare.net/garden13.htm

41. Geothermal heater
http://www1.eere.energy.gov/geothermal/
http://www.geoexchange.org/
http://www.nextenergysolutions.com/

42. Outdoor lighting
http://www.darksky.org/

43. Smart plants
http://www.nrcs.usda.gov/feature/backyard/watercon.html

44. Sprinklers
http://www.safelawns.org/articles/Lawns_and_Your_Carbon_Fo
otprint.ph
http://earthobservatory.nasa.gov/Study/Lawn/lawn3.html
Stoyke, *The Carbon Buster's Home Energy Handbook*
http://www.dwrcymru.com/English/library/publications/DIY%20
Water%20Audit%20(School)/index.asp

46. Lawn and garden chemicals
http://www.organiclawncaretips.com/
http://www.thegreenguide.com/doc/121/lawn

47. Green roof
Estates Gazette, Green shoots. July 14, 2007
Gomez K. Green roofs find favour; Deborah Singerman
explores the green art of vegetating roofs. *Building Product
News* 10 Volume 00, Issue 00, July 1, 2007
Barkham P. G2: Ethical living. The green green grass of home
The Guardian, July 26, 2007

48. Lawnmowers
http://www.peoplepoweredmachines.com/faq-environment.htm

PART THREE
49. New fuel
http://www.businessweek.com/autos/content/may2006/bw200
60508_184780.htm
Giles J. Can biofuels rescue American prairies? Yes, say
ecologists, but not if the current enthusiasm for corn ethanol
continues to hold sway. *New Scientist*, August 18, 2007
http://www.iowacorn.org/ethanol/ethanol_3a.html#environment
http://www.ksgrains.com/ethanol/useth.html
Hoffman B G. Ethanol nation; Brazil finds energy freedom with
sugar-based fuel. *The Detroit News*, August 23, 2007

50. Bike it
http://travel.nytimes.com/2007/10/14/travel/14Journeys.html
Orndorff A. Setting a Course For a Healthier Way of Living.
The Washington Post, July 26, 2007

51. Take the subway
http://www.apta.com/research/info/online/twenty_first_century.cfm
http://www.soundtransit.org/x6043.xml
http://usmayors.org/brownfields/library/PUB_T18.pdf

52. Ditch the car
Beirne M. Temporary Plates. *Brandweek*, July 8, 2007
http://www.eia.doe.gov/emeu/rtecs/chapter3.html

53. Driving aggressively
http://www.edmunds.com/advice/fueleconomy/articles/106842/
article.html
http://www.greenercars.org/drivingtips.htm
http://observer.guardian.co.uk/quiz/questions/0,,1763981,00.html

54. Carpool
http://www.carshare.com
http://www.time.com/time/specials/2007/environment/article/0,2
8804,1602354_1603074_1603736,00.html

55. Idling
http://www.cleangreencars.co.uk/
http://www.edmunds.com/advice/fueleconomy/articles/106842/
article.html
http://alternativefuels.about.com/od/vehiclemaintenanceguide/a/
dieselcoldweath.htm
http://busbuilding.com/bus-conversion/diesel-engine-idling-
from-an-authority-detroit-diesel/

56. Large car
http://www.carpages.co.uk/co2/
http://www.energystar.gov/index.cfm?c=energy_awareness.bus
_energy_use
http://www.fueleconomy.gov
http://www.targetneutral.com,

57. Fewer short trips
http://www.fueleconomy.gov
http://www.vcacarfueldata.org.uk

58. Jetsetting
http://www.time.com/time/specials/2007/environment/article/0,2
8804,1602354_1603074_1603225,00.html
Boston G. The green tour bus; globetrotters striving to
minimize footprint. *The Washington Times*, August 26 2007

59. Use cruise control
http://www.edmunds.com/advice/fueleconomy/articles/106842/
article.html
http://environment.independent.co.uk/green_living/article286698
3.ece
http://www.millbrook.co.uk/

60. Clean and maintain car
http://www.carcare.org/BCCA_service_schedule.pdf

61. Speeding
http://www.greenercars.org/drivingtips.htm
http://www.edmunds.com/advice/fueleconomy/articles/106842/
article.html

62. New tires
http://www.fsec.ucf.edu/en/consumer/transportation/conservati
on/index.htm

63. Walking bus
ELLIS Publications EU White and Green Papers Database.
White Paper on A Strategy for Europe on Nutrition, Overweight
and Obesity related health issues. May 30, 2007

64. Air conditioner
http://www.fsec.ucf.edu/en/consumer/transportation/conservati
on/index.htm

65. Hybrid cars
http://www.carpages.co.uk/co2/

66. Diesel
http://www.clean-diesel.org/images/DPLabelFacts121406.pdf
http://www.cppi.ca/ULSD_Q_A_s.html
http://www.paypershop.com/news-cat2/taxrel141.html

67. Biodiesel
http://www.biodiesel.org
http://www.ers.usda.gov/AmberWaves/September07/Features/
Ethanol.htm
http://www.iowadnr.com/energy/renewable/biodiesel.html
http://www.nzherald.co.nz/section/1/story.cfm?c_id=1&ObjectID
=10381404
http://www.piribo.com/publications/biotechnology/biofuel_marke
t_worldwide_2006.html
http://illumin.usc.edu/article.php?articleID=129&page=2
http://www.vegetableexpert.co.uk/

PART FOUR
68. Recycle cartridges
http://www.cartridgeworldusa.com/section.aspx?id=6984
http://www.worldchanging.com/archives/003767.htm

69. Telecommute
http://www.ce.org/Press/CurrentNews/press_release_detail.asp
?id=11350
http://www.csmonitor.com/2007/0201/p08s02-comv.html
http://www.reason.org/ps338.pdf

70. Junk mail

http://www.biggreenswitch.co.uk/waste_reduction/cancel-junk-mail

http://www.junkbusters.com

71. Reusable container

http://www.platypushydration.com

http://www.slate.com/id/2172541/pagenum/all/

72. CRT computer monitors

http://www.bestbuy.com/site/olspage.jsp?guideID=1110265956484&categoryRep=abcat0500000&type=page&id=cat12077

http://michaelbluejay.com/electricity/howmuch.html

http://www.tellmeaboutcomputers.com/What_Is_A_Computer_Monitor.html

73. Office lighting

http://www.cibse.org/index.cfm?go=page.view&item=599

http://www.coventry.gov.uk/ccm/content/city-services-directorate/public-protection/environmental-health/sustainabledevelopment/switch-it-off-campaign/saving-energy-at-work.en;jsessionid=bcOAPTUj02i-

74. Online newspapers

Hartman J K. Assessing '*USA Today*' As 25th Anniversary Approaches *Editor & Publisher*, September 5, 2007, http://www.editorandpublisher.com/eandp/news/article_display.jsp?vnu_content_id=1003640319, http://zerofootprint.net/blogs/781

76. Reduce your commute

http://abcnews.go.com/Technology/Traffic/story?id=485098&page=1

http://www.ridetowork.org/transportation-fact-sheet

http://www.sciammind.com/article.cfm?articleID=0000DB5A-5A22-132F-949983414B7F0000

http://www.time.com/time/specials/2007/environment/article/0,28804,1602354_1603074_1631489,00.html

77. Single-sided copying

http://www.cibse.org/index.cfm?go=page.view&item=599

http://www.energystar.gov/index.cfm?c=bulk_purchasing.bus_purchasing#off

78. Switch off lights

http://www.cibse.org/index.cfm?go=page.view&item=599

79. Machines on standby

http://www.energysavingtrust.org.uk/aboutest/news/pressreleases/index.cfm?mode=view&press_id=451

80. Lose the ties

http://ergo.human.cornell.edu/Conferences/EECE_IEQ%20and%20Productivity_ABBR.pdf

http://www.npr.org/templates/story/story.php?storyId=14024250

http://yaleglobal.yale.edu/display.article?id=9680

PART FIVE

81. Takeout

http://living.scotsman.com/index.cfm?id=755902006

http://noimpactman.typepad.com/

http://www.nytimes.com/2007/03/22/garden/22impact.html?_r=1&8dpc&oref=slogin

82. Grow your own

Buchan U. Bliss, indeed. *The Spectator*, July 13, 2002

http://www.foe-scotland.org.uk

Hunter L. From puritanical to pleasurable: Potage not as challenging or exotic as it sounds. *National Post*, June 19, 2004

http://seedypeople.co.uk

http://www.vegetableexpert.co.uk/

83. Plastic bags

http://news.bbc.co.uk/2/hi/uk_news/6744105.stm

http://news.nationalgeographic.com/news/2003/09/0902_030902_plasticbags.html

http://www.alternet.org/environment/61607/

http://www.boston.com/news/local/articles/2007/04/26/plastic_bags_may_be_banned_in_boston/?page=2

http://www.cbc.ca/technology/story/2007/03/28/sanfrancisco-plastic.html

http://www.pacia.org.au/index.cfm?menuaction=mem&mmid=009&mid=009.002

http://query.nytimes.com/gst/fullpage.html?res=950DE3DC1738F936A15753C1A96F948260

http://www.reusablebags.com/facts.php

84. Paper towel

http://www.bir.org/aboutrecycling/index.asp

http://www.eia.doe.gov/kids/energyfacts/saving/recycling/solidwaste/paperandglass.html#paper

http://nationalzoo.si.edu/Publications/GreenTeam/

http://www.paperrecycles.org/paper_environment/index.html

http://www.treehugger.com/files/2007/05/lca_handdryer_papertowels.php

85. Recycle paper

http://www.bir.org/aboutrecycling/index.asp

http://www.eia.doe.gov/kids/energyfacts/saving/recycling/solidwaste/paperandglass.html#paper

http://www.paperrecycles.org/paper_environment/index.html

86. Local food

http://www.bbc.co.uk/food/food_matters/foodmiles.shtml

http://www.leopold.iastate.edu/pubs/staff/files/food_travel072103.pdf

87. Plastic cutlery

http://healthychild.org/resources/chemical-pop/bisphenol_a/

http://news.bbc.co.uk/2/hi/science/nature/1734289.stm

http://www.epa.gov/ord/researchaccomplishments/dioxin.html

http://www.greenpeace.org/international/campaigns/toxics/polyvinyl-chloride/the-poison-plastic

http://www.usatoday.com/news/health/2005-04-14-leaching-chemical_x.htm

http://zender-engr.net/docs/health_effects_burning_trash.pdf

88. Corn plastic

http://healthychild.org/resources/article/is_there_a_healthier_plastic_container/

http://www.moneyweek.com/file/32154/profit-from-the-growth-in-green-packaging.html

http://www.smithsonianmag.com/science-nature/10022381.html

89. Bottled water

http://www.connectcarbon.co.uk

http://greenoptions.com/2007/06/20/lighter_footstep_5_reasons_not_to_drink_bottled_water

http://www.macleans.ca/article.jsp?content=20070514_105163_105163

90. Vintage fashion

http://www.re-shirt.net/learnmore

http://www.satradingco.org/Reports/LCA_Final.pdf

http://www.timberland.com/include/csr_reports/2006_TBL_CSR_Report_Full.pdf

91. Disposable diapers

http://www.channel4.com/news/articles/society/environment/factcheck+rash+verdict+on+nappies/603782

http://www.mindfully.org/Plastic/Diaper-Not-Clear.htm

http://www.mothering.com/articles/new_baby/diapers/politics.html
O'Mara P. A tale of two diapers. *Mothering Magazine*, September 1, 2006

http://www.mothering.com/guest_editors/quiet_place/138.html
 Being Green; Buy local. Bring a mug. Hang your laundry. Make repairs. Ride a bike. Use cloth bags. Citizen readers share strategies on 'living lightly'. *The Ottawa Citizen*, May 6, 2007
Watson T. Disposables or cloth? Environment weighs heavily on diaper decisions. *The Seattle Times*, November 4, 2006

92. Cheeseburgers

http://www.openthefuture.com/2006/12/the_footprint_of_a_cheeseburge.html

93. Organic food

http://www.guardian.co.uk/food/Story/0,,1863457,00.html

http://news.bbc.co.uk/2/hi/business/6973352.stm

95. Organic cotton

http://www.drought.nsw.gov.au/reader/soilpak-cotton/csp-b11.pdf

96. Pre-packaged lunches

http://www.carbondetectives.org.uk/content/home/toolkit/foodanddrink

http://nationalzoo.si.edu/Publications/GreenTeam/

97. Green wedding

http://www.greenkarat.com/

http://www.grist.org/advice/possessions/2003/05/08/

http://www.handmadepaper.org.uk/environment-friendly.html

http://www.nodirtygold.org/goldenrules.cfm

http://www.nytimes.com/2007/02/11/fashion/11green.html?pagewanted=2&_r=1

http://www.portovert.com

http://www.soundvision.com/info/weddings/statistics.asp

http://www.treehugger.com/files/2007/04/how-to-green-your-wedding.php

98. Library books

http://www.penguin.co.uk/static/cs/uk/0/aboutus/greenpenguin/whatwecandotohelp.html

http://www.stopglobalwarming.org

99. Extra packaging

http://www.ci.davis.ca.us/pw/recycle/wastereduction.cfm

http://www.epa.gov/garbage/facts.htm

European Environment Agency, Generation and recycling of packaging waste (CSI 017) Assessment http://eea.eu.int

http://thomas.loc.gov

http://www.netregs.gov.uk/netregs/275207/275453/

http://themes.eea.europa.eu/IMS/ISpecs/ISpecification20041007131825/IAssessment1183042279397/view_content

US Environmental Protection Agency. Municipal Solid Waste Generation, Recycling and Disposal in the United States: Facts and Figures for 2003

http://www.vitalgraphics.net/waste2/download/pdf/VWG2_p14and15.pdf

http://www.worldchanging.com/archives/007293.html

100. Carbon offsets

Davies N. The inconvenient truth about the carbon offset industry. *The Guardian,* June 16, 2007
Collinson P. Offset schemes: Why it's harder than you think to pay for a carbon guilt trip. *The Guardian*, February 17, 2007

Index